The Saints of Zara

The Saints of Zara

An Intimate Memoir

ISABEL-ROSE KULSKI

This book is a work of non-fiction. Unless otherwise noted, the author and the publisher make no explicit guarantees as to the accuracy of the information contained in this book and in some cases, names of people and places have been altered to protect their privacy.

Archway Publishing books may be ordered through booksellers or by contacting:

Archway Publishing
1663 Liberty Drive
Bloomington, IN 47403
www.archwaypublishing.com
1 (888) 242-5904

Because of the dynamic nature of the Internet, any web addresses or links contained in this book may have changed since publication and may no longer be valid. The views expressed in this work are solely those of the author and do not necessarily reflect the views of the publisher, and the publisher hereby disclaims any responsibility for them.

ISBN: 978-1-4808-6898-4 (sc)
ISBN: 978-1-4808-6899-1 (hc)
ISBN: 978-1-4808-6897-7 (e)

Library of Congress Control Number: 2018912323

Print information available on the last page.

Archway Publishing rev. date: 10/18/2018

Isabel-Rose Kulski (the author), leaving Zara, August 25, 1962.

Contents

Photographs

Acknowledgments

Photos of Zara, Turkey, are courtesy of Dr. Julian E. Kulski.
The remaining images are from my family files.
Ms. Jane MacDuff and Ms. Ilona Reichenbach helped
me beyond measure to produce this project.

Arrangements

Last night I saw my mother and her cousin Arick lamenting over ghosts that belong to another time and world. I had never imagined them as anything except as I saw them there—middle-aged, ordinary, tired women in faded, flowery housedresses. And then it dawned on me they had once been young and full of dreams—perhaps possessing the same fervor I felt about my own future back in the innocent year of 1940. I suppose dreams of the years when one is young are the hardest to forget, because I noticed that when the two women spoke, their dark eyes filled with tears and their voices became peculiarly throaty. I cannot say when I became aware I was listening, for I had heard the same stories many times and had thought them utterly boring. But this time it seemed different—not just a history of somebody's past but an imprint of a life on a scroll of time.

My mother could never look upon the past without tearful regret that those precious dreams of youth had left behind them only phantoms to haunt her. She always felt that hers was a special kind of tragedy that scarred her future as well as her past. I knew she had had a singularly hard life, but as I heard her talking that evening with her friend, I began to see that there were others before her and still others before them whose lives had been a tortuous complexity of history.

They came from a little place called Zara in the "old country" where they grew up, and I could hear both the nostalgia and the hollowness in their voices as they talked of a life that was gone forever. Often when I am at my studies or reading, I will look up from my books and see my mother staring at the floor or out into the distance, completely oblivious to everything around her. I wonder what she thinks about. Perhaps she is again a young girl, running wildly through the hills covered with tall grasses and flowers, her dark hair loosely flying behind her. Or maybe she has forgotten all that and thinks of other things I know nothing of—of marriage and birth and life and death, of whole families and villages that have disappeared.

That summer evening, her cousin Arick talked of her youth and the things she had hoped for that were lost with the years. She said something about her own children—how she would never interfere with their lives when they wanted to marry. And then she recalled a scene of an older man whom her father had taken on as a kind of ward or helper and had decided he could be even more useful as a husband for his daughter. That was the way marriages were arranged then in that far-off country. The poor girl was only fifteen, just a little brat, she said, and she didn't want to marry anyone and certainly not this shy, friendless man with an old-looking face and a large, graying mustache. I remember particularly her saying she spent that night on the damp, cold earth of a cellar, naked and praying she would die.

Arick didn't marry that man, but years later, when her parents found her still on their hands, they (or she) selected another man—a handsome but awkward youth. He was another of my mother's cousins who had grown up in her household. "You're ugly," Arick quoted her mother as saying. "If you don't take this one, there will be no other." Even though the ensuing marriage brought forth many children, Arick seemed not entirely reconciled to her fate. Perhaps I am wrong, but that is how it appeared to me that evening. I noticed the muscles around her eyes twitched, and I thought she was going to cry. But she had more endurance than my mother. She said something about mistakes others make for us.

Then they began to talk about the reject, the "old man," of how no one had wanted to marry him and of how my mother was finally forced into it by her relatives who had taken her with them to America. She never learned to like this old man, as she called him—love was not even a concept—for besides his clumsy appearance, he had no redeeming attributes to attract her. I could tell by the way she talked that she still revolted against him, though they had been apart many years. I thought I perceived sympathy and tolerance when Arick spoke, but perhaps it was only pity that came after the years had passed. Arick talked of his youth—he was an orphan; of how her own father had treated him like a servant when he was still a boy; of his shyness, his uncomplaining forbearance, his subservience. She said he had been friendless all his life. No one had ever liked him, and yet he was the best of the good men. She was talking about my father.

The Old Country: Nishan's Story

After I got to know something of my father's history, I realized that the portrait the two women had drawn that evening was quite accurate. "The best of the good men," Arick had said. His name was Nishan. He was born in Zara, a town on the old Roman Road going east from what today is Ankara, Turkey. Zara had about five thousand inhabitants when I saw it in 1962; they were Turkish, except for a few forlorn Armenians who were like people left behind after a great flood or hurricane, alone but clinging to their identity. But in 1875, the year my father was born, the town must have been larger. Perhaps half of the inhabitants were Armenian.

There were three brothers—Manoog, Artin, and Minas. Their father was Garabed Gagian. He was a merchant who carried goods from the Black Sea port of Trebizond across the mountains, the plains, and the Taurus Range to Damascus, Syria—bales of linen, metalwork, and other things. He brought back rugs, spices, and tobacco. When he died, he is said to have left thirty bales of linen at two hundred pounds each in Trebizond. He must have traveled hundreds, perhaps thousands of miles over rocky cliffs and parched earth in his lifetime, but that is the only imprint of his life that is left for me.

Manoog, his oldest son, married Oghida, from the Sherinian

family in Zara. That was the surname of Arick, the cousin of my mother. Arick and my father were related by marriage and, as I later learned, by blood as well. My mother said that Armenians, according to the edict of their religion, had to be seven steps removed from a relative before marriage was permitted. Arick and Nishan were closer than that, so perhaps that was one reason for her rejection of him— but if so, why did her father push her toward him? In the new country of America, there was evidently no other of their kind to marry.

Manoog and Oghida, his wife, moved to the town of Gurin, about a hundred miles south of Zara in the Taurus Mountains, where Oghida's mother, who was from the Tickmen family, lived. They had a boy, Nishan (my father), but Oghida died when the boy was barely a year old. Manoog then left the boy with his grandmother, himself returning to his brothers in Zara. Nishan's middle name was Manoog, after his father. He said he remembered his father a little, as he had made a return visit to Gurin, riding a black horse. He had remarried.

Some years later, on a summer day, the three brothers, Manoog, Artin, and Minas, walked out of Zara to work in a little village called Devutsa. "On the way," said Nishan in a slim memoir he wrote for me, "they rested. Manoog fell asleep. His brothers said, 'Manoog, get up; let's go.' He did not pay attention. A scorpion had bitten him on the neck. The brothers brought him back to Zara, where he died."

Manoog's new wife, having no contact with little Nishan in Gurin, subsequently married someone else, taking with her whatever worldly goods, if any, Manoog had left behind. So Nishan was in the sole care of the Gurin grandmother. He called her Ana, also Mother. She was a religious woman, devoted to the local Armenian church.

A Wandering Childhood

Gurin, "Yeshil Gurin" (green Gurin), the Turks called it—and when I saw it, the green was emerald, made brighter by the stark white clay and sandy land that surrounded it. High limestone cliffs, pock-marked by ancient cave openings, circled the valley, and fresh water gushed down to a river that ran through the town and eventually became a tributary to the Euphrates. There were fruit trees, apricots mostly, in the small orchards throughout the town. Here Nishan spent his early youth with his grandmother, Ana Tickmen.

In his memoir, Nishan says,

> A widow, Ana made her living weaving wool. I used to take it to a person who made carpets, bringing back more wool for weaving. This person had four sheep who gave both wool and milk. During Lent, a seven-week period, he kept the milk to make cheese, which would be ripe by Easter. It was used in the church service along with eggs. In the service, when the priest would say, "Arek, gerek" ("take and eat," symbolizing the body of Christ), we hungry boys would take the food outside, sit in the sun beside the church's stone walls, and eat.
>
> Tickmen Ana had mulberries and when they were ripe in June I would climb the tree and shake it. We would put a sheet under the tree to catch the berries. They were put into a big brass pot and cooked, along with the flies that took their fill of the sweet syrup. This mixture, when cooled, was squeezed and pressed through a thin cloth to make molasses, *bekmez*. This was made into little balls, dried in the sun on the roof, and kept in containers for food for the sheep in the winter. Every fall the village people killed sheep. The man who did the coating of brasspots did the slaughtering. He used to make *ghaourma* (browned meat pieces), put in spices, mould it, and put a string through it. It would be hung in the attic to eat in winter. It was very tasty.

Nishan was sent to a church school; whether the school was Protestant or Orthodox Armenian is unclear.

> We had a man teacher from Marash, who came to school on a white donkey. I began to learn to read and write.

I remember in 1888 we had another teacher who came from Sivas to Gurin. He taught us Turkish: "Long live my prince," etc. Alas, those beautiful days when the mind was strong!

This teacher taught us school discipline. They used to put you on your back and tie your feet. Two boys would lift your feet and the teacher would hit with a cane. While he was hitting the boys would say,

Why are you lying down, dear friend?
Now you can have a hundred lashes
So that your brain will come back
To you from your feet.
Why don't you listen to the teacher?
When he says something?

Then one day, when Nishan was twelve, Ana Tickmen got sick. It was spring. Her friends came to find out how she was.

"I went in and moved her head. She does not wake up," I said. The ladies came in and said she was dead. They notified the church. The elders came in and made a list of all she had. It was given to the head of the church. So I was left alone.

Orphaned now for a second time, homeless, and destitute, "They gave me to Hagop," Nishan recalls. Hagop was the son of Ana Tickmen's brother, so he was Nishan's uncle once removed. So, for the next few years, Nishan was in this household, where there were several children.

They had much work. I did what they told me—bring water, chop wood and so on.

There was a dispute between Hagop and one Chulbash over some land along the river. It was taken to court, and it appears the Chulbash side won. It is not at all clear why Nishan now ended up in the Chulbash household. Perhaps it was part of the settlement of the dispute. Hagop may have been tired of taking care of this boy and had agreed that Chalbash could take him. But was there a consideration? Who knows what contrivances occurred among people living in such a fragile society?

> I was a servant for three years at Chulbash's. In the fall they gave me new clothes. I didn't get any pay.

1895, a Fateful Year

In the fall of 1895, there was an upheaval the Ottoman government could not or did not want to control. Westerners living in Turkey at the time—missionaries and teachers—were among the victims. Their numerous accounts attest to the violence and lawlessness that ravaged the whole country. Many wrote that it was sanctioned, even instigated, by Sultan Abdul Hamid II.

Nishan was now nineteen. He had spent his childhood and youth in Gurin as an orphan boy after his grandmother's death, wandering here and there as a servant to earn his bread and board, such as they might be. When the troubles began, Nishan writes,

> Most of us fled to the rocky caves in the hills around Gurin. Twelve of us went in hiding with our priest. The Turkish mob found us and yelled, *"Selavet, Gueterin,"* and we raised our arms in surrender. "Obey the orders." The Turks came near and hit us one by one. They hit me, too, but I was not hurt. I had a few coins. "Here, sir," I said. "I have *para* [money]." Two or three I hid in the ground. Shortly another group arrived. There are three or four of us now behind the rocks. They shouted, "Surrender." We came forth. I was at the edge of the group. I changed my place and went to join the others. Those wicked people came and hit the priest and a boy with their guns. Thus, because I had moved away, the Lord kept me.

Now it was dark. I was left with no clothes. I found a piece of burlap and covered myself. We came below to the town from our hiding place. A few Turkish neighbors and Turkish outlaws joined them. Quietly we passed barefoot—we had not shoes—and made our way to the mill.

In the fall every home gleans its wheat for the whole year and carries it to the mill. We went there. What do you think we saw? Flour, wheat all mixed up. The Turks had cut the bags and carried them away. I wanted to go with my friend. His brother and someone else were killed, along with their wives.

A river runs through the town of Gurin

We were told that the *Hodja* (Turkish holy man) was going to gather all the Armenians together and hand us over to the government. He did so the next morning. The government office is three miles away. Hodja took a white cloth and make a banner, attaching it to a stick, and we followed him. Some were wounded. Turks and Kurds in groups met us. The killed and wounded were left behind. The girls they took away and also killed some others.

Finally the *Hodja* led us in the garden of the government office. Again some Turks and savage Kurds entered the enclave to kill. There was a Turk who sent a telegram to the governor of Sivas province. An order came back that peace had been declared. Thus we survived. We were camped in the government compound. They cooked some pilaf (cracked wheat) for us. The next day they let us out.

The hill caves surrounding the town of Gurin

Winter passed. In March, part of Chulbash's house burned. We renovated it. When they dug the burnt area out to see what there was, a Turk came and tried to frighten us with a gun. I ran away. The Turk took what he liked.

In the Chulbash household there now gathered seven or eight children around five or six years old. Three brothers and their wives lived together. There was a child one year in age. I think her name was Margaret. When she cried at night I used to rock her. I remember one day I hit her with my fingers. The mother was very angry. How lucky I was that God did not break my fingers.

The mulberries ripened. We had to bring them in to cook in order to make molasses. We had much work that summer.

This is Nishan's stark account of the 1895 turmoil that shook the whole of Turkey. More was to follow.

Clara Barton's Mission[1]

My father's memoir is but a thin sliver of the events of that year, 1895. Internal unrest had erupted like an epidemic throughout the interior of Turkey, and news of the violent attacks of Muslims—Turks and Kurds—on Christian minorities, mainly Armenians, had reached the Western world. Many American religious denominations had for years established and maintained missionary stations and churches in Turkey, and concern for their own people as well as for the local Christian populations had aroused the attention of prominent Americans.

Among them was Clara Barton, who, as head of the American Red Cross, was one of the great humanitarian voices of the nineteenth century. Responding to public demand in America to do something to help the suffering Christians of Turkey, she organized a mission to go there to see for herself what had happened and to do the work of resuscitation. She was seventy years old, with her already illustrious career behind her, but neither age nor lack of foreign experience deterred her. The American Red Cross up to that point had not fielded a mission abroad.

The Turkish Minister in Washington refused to grant her or the Red Cross permission to enter Turkey, even though Turkey, along with the great powers of the day, had adhered to the establishment of an International Red Cross organization in 1865. Undaunted, she got a team together and, with financing through contributions from the American public, set out for Constantinople, reaching there in July 1896, when Western newspapers reported accounts of starvation following the mass killings of the previous fall and winter. Her reputation in the world was such that she went straight to the minister

---

[1] Information in this section is from *Report, American Relief Expedition to Asia Minor under the Red Cross*. Washington, DC, 1896. Permission granted by the Office of the General Council, American Red Cross, W.D.C., November 10, 2017. (In the public domain.)

of foreign affairs. Through a promise of impartiality as to Muslims and Christians, as well as a veiled warning that the "civilized world" would be aroused if she were refused, she got the minister, who spoke for the sultan, to agree to allow her team of Red Cross volunteers, by now consisting of five separate groups, to go into the provinces to do their work.

These small field expeditions were made up of educators, doctors, missionaries, and Red Cross officials, who mapped out separate routes to reach the interior towns and villages on the Anatolian plateau. Conditions of travel and communication were primitive, even for that time. Over much of the area, there was no land route but only "pony posts" like the overland days in California. The way was infested with brigands; there were no regular passenger boats for the Black Sea coastal route. It took at least six weeks to get mail from Constantinople to the interior. Only the largest towns had the telegraph, and it took anywhere from two days to a week to get a telegram through, all such dispatches being sent and answered in Turkish only. The larger towns had mail leaving usually once a week under military guard. No newspaper was published in Asia Minor. The missionary stations were not near the sea coast, and it took from three to fifteen days to travel to them from the Mediterranean or Black Sea ports. Inland towns were nearly inaccessible in winter and early spring. So wrote Miss Barton in her report at the conclusion of the mission.

Excerpts from the reports attributed to Miss Barton by each of these teams give a pretty good picture of what they encountered and what they did:

After facing rain, snow and wind for three days, we came to **Marash.** Typhus, dysentery, and smallpox were spreading as a result of the awful crowded state of the city. Marash had been filled with refugees since the November massacres, notwithstanding that a large part of its own dwelling houses had been burned and plundered. The surrounding country had also been pillaged, people killed and villages destroyed, and the frightened remnant of people had crowded in here for protection ... preachers requested mothers not to bring children with smallpox to church; nevertheless typhus and smallpox spread. By the efforts of the wives of the missionaries a hospital had been established with plenty of patients, but they had no funds for physicians or medicines. Medicines were left and funds furnished a native Armenian doctor educated in America.

* * *

Nearly the entire city of **Arabkir** was in ruins; only heaps of stones where houses had been. Out of 1,800 homes but few remained, the markets as well as the dwellings were destroyed, and people, plundered and destitute, were crowded into the few remaining houses, down with typhus. We were told that six hundred had already died of the disease, and the people's physician, the only one in that part of the country, was in prison.

* * *

Approaching **Killis**, rumors came to us of troubles in that city, and when we reached there, openly menaced and looted by the rabble, we found the ill news only too true. An uprising had taken place in the city, many people were slain, and the shops and households had been plundered ... Leaving **Killis** ... our long caravan strung out single file over the foothills and into the mountains, a brave sight and one I am sure that, could they have seen it, would have delighted the hearts of the charitable Americans, whose contributions were finding a way to the desolated homes of Anatolia. The trail was tortuous and muddy and for much of the way among huge boulders up and down over mountains and valleys—uninhabitable, treeless, stony wastes. For miles the only signs of human life were bands of Kurds or wandering Gypsies, and flocks of cattle, sheep and goats, with the wild-looking skin-clad shepherds who led them in search of the scanty herbage that grows in the springtime among this chaos of rocks, a weird, monotonous country, a wilderness and the picture of desolation.

* * *

Two long days in the saddle ... brought us to the ancient city of **Diarbekir** ... Everywhere from the neighborhood, refugees had fled into the city ... As we approached we passed several burned and deserted villages where every house had been looted. Although about two thousand people were killed in the city itself and a whole quarter of the bazaars laid waste and everyone plundered, yet the loss was proportionally much less than in the surrounding villages, which had been sacked of every portable thing they possessed, even to the doors, floors and timbers on the roofs ... Thirty-seven hundred shops destroyed.

* * *

Malatia depends largely on trade with the Kurdish villages ... The Christian population go to them for business. Some sow grain, others do carpentry work, shoemaking and the like. Since the events of last November (1895) all intercourse has been stopped because of the hostile attitude of these villages toward the Christians ... We found 1,883 orphans and 650 widows. The widows we supplied with spinning wheels by which they can earn something, though not enough to support a family. Miss Harris (missionary) has taken samples of embroideries, for which she hopes to find a market in Europe. Of houses there were 567 burned, and the people are now living in the gardens, but the Armenian Relief Committee in Constantinople has given funds to aid in rebuilding ... Artisans have been supplied with tools ... and to one village we gave twenty oxen.

* * *

Our particular efforts were to save the great grain crop of the **Harpoot** plain ... the one bar ... against famine in the future ... If the grain crop could not be properly harvested and secured the number of ragged and starving would be woefully augmented ... It was our purpose to lift the people up from their deplorable ruins.

* * *

The total contribution to the Red Cross for this mission, the Barton report said, amounted to $116,000 (in then-current terms), and except for traveling expenses of the agents, the money went to help prevent starvation; to care for the sick; to buy clothes, thread, pins, and needles; seeds, agricultural implements, and oxen for the farmers; tools for the blacksmiths and carpenters; looms for weavers. The great want beyond this initial aid was for material to help people rebuild their burned and ruined homes and villages.

The report speaks of the villages sending out welcoming committees to greet the agents and of the gratitude of the populations for their mission. Beyond that, the report said,

> The Red Cross agents have ... gathered a great stock of information about the massacres and the awful abuse of girls and women; as unimpeachable witnesses, they can bear testimony to the frightful sufferings and needs of the people. We must sincerely hope and pray that Miss Barton and the agents and friends of the Red Cross will not esteem their work in Turkey done but ... will bend every effort to secure further relief for the widows and orphans of the more than sixty-thousand murdered men—mostly between the ages of eighteen and fifty—whose lives no earthly arm was outstretched to save.
>
> (—a testimonial in the Barton Report from Rev. Joseph K. Greene, Constantinople. That figure was greatly multiplied later by the reports of devastation and starvation.)

From my father's memoir, it is evident he had no conception, either at the time or later, of the extent of the destruction throughout the interior of the country or any suspicion that the government may have been a party to allowing it, as historians later wrote. He stayed in Gurin for another six years, doing odd jobs that came to hand to survive. The Red Cross report mentioned Sivas as a stop where seed grain was left. There is no mention of either Gurin or Zara, so these towns may not have had the good fortune to receive this generous American help. But there is also an official record, made by reporting consular officers of the great powers (Britain, France, Russia, Germany, and others) as well as America, attesting to the murderous upheavals across Turkey.

The Road to Zara

The year is 1901. Nishan is now twenty-six years old. Orphaned at an early age, he has lost his one close relative in Gurin, his grandmother Ana Tickmen, who was a mother to him. He has been shunted from place to place, working as a youth apparently just for his food and a place to sleep. He learned enough at the church school to be literate, but he has no education, has not been apprenticed to anyone to learn a trade, and seems to be a lost soul. He has barely survived the upheaval and killings by Turks and their mercenaries, the Kurds, that shook the villages of Turkey in 1895 and closed down the foreign missionary establishments. He doesn't know, nor do the Armenians in the provinces of the eastern part of Turkey, that the once all-powerful Ottoman Empire, that had had a certain tenuous modus vivendi with its minorities, has been greatly weakened in the world and blackened for its barbaric treatment of its citizens, especially the Armenians. There is no hope in Gurin for such a young man. So, one day he tells this "Agha" he serves that he is leaving and going to find his way north to Sivas, to the place of his birth, Zara, where his father had died and where he may be fortunate enough to find some surviving relatives. That is his only remaining refuge now.

The trip to Sivas from Gurin is about one hundred miles. I made it by car in two hours in 1962, but it took Nishan three days on foot. He had to traverse Kurdish territory. The Kurds were still in some of the villages in my time. The road lies below the rise of the Taurus Range, and in the late-summer afternoon, the women were threshing grain, circling stone wheels that threw up the shafts, which were caught in the flickering golden light, their bright-colored clothes and dark visages flashing against the chalky background of the hills. There was no violence in the 1960s. Turkey had become a US ally, one might even say a dependent, at least in a military sense, and the threat of violence hovered potentially to the east, beyond the border, from the Soviet Union.

Nishan's road to Zara was slow. First he went to Sivas, a town clanking with the hammering of metalworkers. In Nishan's time, it seemed to be something of an artisans' hub. He describes the job he found as an electroplater.

> In Sivas I went to work in the house of the Touajam. I was a servant—went to market to shop for food. They gave me money and sometimes I would steal some of it. I am so sad thinking about it since that was such a good family. And yet they loved me. They always advised me to be good. They were rich. We had lots of water, but not good for drinking. I used to bring the drinking water in huge pitchers on my shoulders.
>
> One day in the market I met a friend from Zara. He wanted me to go there to see my grandmother from my father's side, Grandma Sherinian. So I went.
>
> I went to stay with my uncle Artin and his wife Donig. They were poor and lived in a single room. My father's share had been made into a stable. Nishan Sherinian advised me to sue them. I gave a small payment to a lawyer and won the suit. There was a man named Sarkis Khenjedian. He

scolded me, saying "Why do we break each other's hearts?" He was a good Christian. Later when I came to America I sent the money back to my uncle's wife so my conscience would be clear.

There were two brothers, Krikor and Mardiros Aghajanian. They were related to my grandmother. They had a rug business and also went to the villages to electroplate pots. They took me with them. All pots and pans at that time were copper, the spoons wood. There were many Armenian platers. Every place we did electroplating we were given something to eat. We used to have two or three portions, depending on the work we did. I used to go and ask for food and bring whatever they gave me—my share.

There was a Turk named Tahih Agha in the village of Boghur, near Zara. He was very rich. He had a wife, two boys, a servant and many animals. When we did their plates Hanum (his wife) gave us good meals. We ate and whatever was left we used to keep. I used to go and bring the pots of this family to clean. These people had a lot of iron utensils. They used to forge them into swords. The pots had iron bases which I used to clean with my feet. Artin, my uncle, would then clean the sides. Pieces of brass would be melted and used to cover the holes.

I stayed a while at my uncle's house, then at another family named Baha. I stayed the winter there. They had a donkey. I used to comb and water it. There were two daughters, Lusig and Sarig. I wanted to marry Lusig but I did not succeed. Sarig wanted to marry me but I did not want her. It is against the law to marry a close relative.

This household got tired of me and gave me a quantity of wheat and put me out to my grandmother's.

So now, with the horrors of 1895 stamped in his memory, his years of wandering as a laborer, his youth slipping away, Nishan in the fall of 1901 finds himself back in Zara, his birthplace, with his father's relatives. He goes to his grandmother's, an elderly lady from the Sherinian clan.

Nishan's Zara relatives

Missionaries and Zara Converts[2]

We must now pause and let Nishan rest a bit while we turn to the Mormon missionaries, to learn how they got to Zara and what they did there.

In the early rise of the Church of Jesus Christ of Latter-Day Saints (hereafter I will use the designation Mormon in referring to the Church), its founding head sent out as a missionary or elder a man named Orson Hyde to Jerusalem to convert the Jews to Christianity. With church doctrine and the Bible as his guide, this first missionary's instruction was to convince the Jews, whose in-gathering to Jerusalem had been much prophesied, that "after they have been scattered and the Lord hath scourged them by other nations, for the space of many generations ... they shall be persuaded to believe in Christ, the Son of God ... and look not forward anymore for another Messiah."

With that impetus, missionaries continued throughout the remainder of the nineteenth century to go to other lands under the rule of the Ottoman Turks to preach their religion. Not being allowed to

---

[2] Permission for use of material in this section, derived from the *Millennial Star*, was granted by the Correlation Intellectual Property, The Church of Jesus Christ of Latter-Day Saints, by email on January 24, 2018.

preach—although they did—among the Muslims, the Mormon missionaries concentrated on the minority non-Muslim populations and in 1888 established a headquarters for what became known as the "Turkish Mission" in Aleppo, Syria. From 1884 to 1900, a total of twenty-seven missionaries, or Elders of Zion as they were known, worked out of Syria, going to the southern provinces of Turkey. A few made their way up to Sivas and thence eastward to the town of Zara, where they found a warm receptivity to their message. Why that particular town and not others along the way is not clear, other than that contact among some adventurous Armenian travelers had been firmly established earlier in Syria. As noted in Nishan's memoir, there was an Armenian trade route between Trebizond on the Black Sea coast and Aleppo, Syria.

> "Our work till now has been mostly among the Armenians, a people in whose veins run the blood of Israel," one of the elders reported back to headquarters in Utah. "Their ancestors were most likely in the line of the northward march of the ten tribes, and very probably associated and mingled with them. Their characteristics point strongly to an infusion of the blood of Reuben, for they are, as was that prince of Israel, 'unstable as water.' They are apt and industrious, yet lack in capacity for leadership, sharp but shallow, shrewd but not sturdy." (*Millennial Star,* April 20, 1902, p. 217)

Did the missionaries, as seems implied here, believe that they were after all having some success in converting "Israelites," which Armenians are not, since they had not had any real success earlier among the Jews? However that may be, success was to be had in the town of Zara. A small colony of "Saints," as they now referred to themselves, was flourishing there, and among them was the head of the Sherinian clan, Nishan, to whom, as I noted earlier, my father, also named Nishan, was related.

The first Mormon missionaries had reached Zara in 1884 from

the Turkish Mission headquarters in Aleppo, Syria. Only a few of their elders actually reached Zara, the others branching out from Aleppo and Aintab. The first Zara contact with the missionaries was by this Nishan Sherinian and companions, who traveled to Syria, evidently as traders. It is unlikely, except for this early encounter, that the Mormons would have gotten to Zara at all. Other Christian denominations (Methodist, Baptist) are mentioned in my mother's oral history before the arrival of the Mormons, but it is rather a puzzle that of all the larger places between Aleppo and Zara, none is recorded as a station receiving these "Saints."

In any event, before 1895, Missionaries Hintze, Booth, Hermann, Woodbury, and perhaps others are all in Zara. As this Nishan Sherinian is of the very same family as my mother's cousin Arick, it may be through him that both sides of my family are now introduced to, and their lives and fortunes affected by, these religious voices from Utah, the "Zion of the West," as the Mormons call their home.

Return of the Missionaries

Year by year, the missionaries reestablished themselves in their old strongholds. On June 9, 1905, Elder Wilford Booth wrote from Gurin to the president of the Church about the "persecutions" the church had suffered in the town of Sivas. (This is the only reference I have found of a visit to Gurin, my father's town.) Noting the "few Saints" living in Zara, he said, "I cannot help longing for a colony for our poor Saints, who need assistance in helping themselves to earn a living."

The situation seemed to improve that summer, as Booth, on July 25, 1905, wrote from Zara: "Mormonism stands in better favor with the people here than at any time previous to this visit." He was even invited to speak at the Gregorian (Armenian Apostolic) Church.

We assembled down by the river's verdant side early yesterday morning with the saints and some invited friends, about seventy in all, and all day long we sported on the green meadow or sat and talked beneath the shadow of gigantic willows; but we did not use them to hang our harps upon, for there was no weeping among us, and we sang the songs of Zion with no restraint of sorrow in our hearts. The children danced around the "maypole"—the first one they ever saw—and wound the strings in piebald braid around the trembling stick; the boys played ball and leap-frog, raced and tumbled over the springy ground; the girls joined in other sports, and numerous were the feats performed, and heartily were they all enjoyed by the aged forms, too feeble now to make the agile step of youth. Prizes were given to the expert in all the games, prizes of pens, pencils, paper, paints, combs, mirrors, and ribbons, and strange to say, every one was given something.

In the afternoon, when the "shadow and the object are equal in length," we ceased our sport, spread out the rugs in the shade by the bank of the river, and assembled there in meeting to sing and pray and preach. When the services were over four persons went with me down into the water and were baptized into the fold, and in a few minutes were confirmed members in the Church of Jesus Christ of Latter-day Saints.

All enjoyed themselves very much, and our friends were cordial in their thanks for the splendid day and program. Rich and poor alike were there, but there were unity and harmony and love. We expect more baptisms in the near future. (*Millennial Star,* August 24, 1905, p.540)

Booth's work was its own reward, for he said the call for the Book of Mormon was great, and when he left on August 23, 1905, the Saints of Zara bade him a tearful farewell.

After a new period of internal disturbances in Turkey in 1909, by 1910, the last of the Zara converts had emigrated. We resume the fate of those left behind in a later section of my account (see Section 10: "In Search of Things Past")

At the time the missionaries found it, Zara was a small town, about half Armenian and half Turkish. It wouldn't be found on most ordinary maps of the region, but it is an old town. Its ancient wooden houses recalled a dying elegance of times gone by—perhaps two or three hundred years—when the town must have been smaller and certainly more prosperous. Most of the people lived in small stone houses with flat roofs sloping down the hillsides and toward the Kizil Irmak, the river that drains the high plateaus and winds its way gradually north to the Black Sea. Zara is on the high plateau, not in the mountains, and except for the ribbon of green that traces the course of the river it is mostly dry, with the hues of red rocks and yellow ochre sandstone. Sheep-raising and wheat or dry farming were the main source of its livelihood. There was a small mosque and a small, ancient Armenian church at the time of the active missionaries, but the town didn't have a well-established missionary college.

Armenians had been scattered throughout Turkey for centuries. As they had their own written language as far back as the fifth century and their own national church going back further to the fourth century, they must have kept records relating to church affairs and members of parishes for generations, but neither of my parents brought with them any such documents when they came to America, though both were literate in Armenian and also spoke Turkish. Zara was more an Armenian than a Turkish town. There were separate Turkish and Armenian cemeteries, mosques, and churches. The head of the local government, the mayor or *Kaimakam*, was most likely Turkish, as would have been the provincial governor. There was a military presence there in the form of the Turkish Third Army, facing the traditional Russian adversary to the east. Farther to the east of Zara, at Erzerum and Kars, historic fortifications stood, and bitter battles had been fought between the Turks and the Russians episodically throughout the nineteenth century. Armenians had lived on both sides of the border, as they had since time immemorial. Their own days of glory having long since expired, they were caught between the contending powers in all directions.

A view of Zara. Hosanna's home was similar to those in the foreground.

Hosanna's Story: Relationships

I now refer to an oral account from Hosanna Kezerian, my mother, and to some genealogy to get a picture of this enclave of Armenians in the town of Zara.

My mother could trace her family through memory and story to her paternal great-grandfather, Kezer Khachkov. "Kezer," she said, means tax collector, which was his job. He would go to the surrounding villages to collect for the government. The family name may have been derived from this Kezer. Before that it was supposedly Badoian. Sarig Aslanian was his wife. One child, Gougas, is on record, but as families were usually numerous, there were no doubt others. Kezer lived, died, and was buried in Zara.

This Gougas is of special interest. The word means "apostate," according to my mother. Before the Mormons came, Gougas took up with Methodist missionaries who were in Zara and sent his children to the small school they had established there. Because of this and his later receptivity of the Mormons, he was buried outside the Armenian cemetery. He was still alive, though, when my mother left Zara; he died in 1912. I was told his grave is marked by a big stone in one of the Kezerian fields on the outskirts of Zara.

Gougas's wife, Gule (Rose) Barsoian, stayed with the Armenian Apostolic Church. Her brother was a "*vartabed*" (priest) who lived at the monastery across the river bordering Zara. She and Gougas had seven children. She died just about the time Hosanna (my mother) left for America in 1910. She was buried in the Armenian cemetery. The children were: Hovhanes (my mother's father), Tatos, Krikor, Khachig (boys), and Sarig, Hegna, and Yagout (girls). My father (Nishan) knew them. He said the boys were all tall and good looking. What happens to this family is a history of those times, and that is why they are introduced individually here.

Now I turn to the immediate forebears of my mother: Hovhanes and his wife Gulvart. We have just sketched Hovhanes's side—the Kezerians. Gulvart came from the Gagosian family—Murat, her father, and Shooshan Avjugian, her mother. My mother remembered them, her maternal grandparents. As children, she and her sister would go to Shooshan's house for special treats. In winter, Shooshan would bring out a ladder and go to the loft to take down dried fruit and walnuts to give them. Shooshan died when Hosanna was seven or eight and was buried in the Armenian cemetery in Zara, perhaps beside her husband Murat, by a spring inside the wall. This was before 1915.

Gougas Kezerian
Hosanna's paternal grandfather
and head of the family in Zara

Hovhanes was born in Zara. He was intelligent and could read and write Armenian and Turkish, as his father, Gougas, had sent him to the Methodist missionary school in Zara. He himself, unlike Gougas, seems not to have been accepting of the missionaries as he grew up. Whether the Mormons converted him I have no record, but he did not want his children (my mother and her brother, Antranig), to go to America when they were sponsored by the Mormon Church.

I do not know whether Gulart

was a convert or what her schooling was. What remnant of her life is recallable becomes an integral and poignant part of this story. She was born in Zara. She and Hovhanes had eight children:

Antranig (meaning firstborn) (boy)
Osanna (my mother, Hosanna)
Ezekial (boy)
Muketar (boy)
Perpion (girl)
Oshooki (girl)
Esahag (boy)
Arshalous (girl)

The last three died in early childhood, Oshooki at age three, Esahag at age four (convulsions), and Arshalous (asphyxiation) as a baby. I wonder if the special hardships after 1895 may have contributed to their deaths. Of the others, their fates are to be told.

Now we go back to the scene in Zara, where my father has returned to his maternal grandmother's people, who are from the same family as Nishan Sherinian, the first in Zara to encounter the Mormon missionaries. These Sherinians, related as they are to my father through his maternal grandmother, are also intertwined as a clan by marriage with my mother's Kezerian clan.

Tatos (one of the four sons of Gougas) marries Felor Sherinian.
Myram (sister of my mother) marries Esahag Sherinian.
Antranig (my mother's brother) marries Lucy Sherinian.

Then there is Arick, daughter of Nishan Sherinian, who marries Armenag Kezerian, the son of one of Gougas's four boys (Khachig). Thus, he is my mother's first cousin, who grew up in her household after his father's death. The rule may have been not to marry a close relative (seven steps removed, according to my mother), but whether by choice or arrangement for lack of an alternative, the Sherinians and Kezerians managed to weave an intricate marital tapestry. They were meshed together in Zara, but the close ties were broken once they are transplanted in America.

Clans: The Sherinians and the Kezerians

This idyllic picture of the Saints of Zara did not encompass all of the members of the families who had embraced the faith or even relations within each family. As was evident with the Kezerians, a source of dissension was the split over religion itself. As noted, old Grandpa Gougas had received the Mormon missionaries in his home, such as it may have been, but at least one of his sons, Hovhanes, rejected them. Hovhanes's absence from the group picture of the Saints is testimony enough of that, and the fact that he rejected the idea of his children following the missionaries to America must have been a cause for quarrelling or silent hostility within the family.

(*See the group picture on final page, "The Saints of Zara."*)

There was tension among the Sherinian clan as well, as my father's memoir shows. As I noted, Nishan, my father, had found his way after years of drifting from family to family and job to job back to Zara, the seat of his father's family, there also to find his fraternal grandmother, Khatounmar Sherinian.

A reversion to genealogy, a passion among the Mormons with a great religious significance, is in order at this point.

The relationship of the two Nishans is this: There was a Sherinian, Sherin, the husband of Khatounmar. He had been born in Zara. He had a brother, Krikor, also born in Zara. This brother was the father of Nishan Sherinian. So, according to my research, the two Nishans were cousins once removed, and Arick and my father, Nishan, third cousins.

The Sherinians were not Zara-bound farmers. Sherin had gone to Constantinople to work as a Han (carrier), one of the lowest and hardest forms of labor in Ottoman society. He had taken with him his son, Lucaref, who contracted dysentery and died in Constantinople, leaving behind two daughters, Lucy and Sarah. Nishan Sherinian, as noted, was the pioneer who steered people of Zara to the Mormons. He and my father, up to this point, had not had much if any contact with each other, but when in 1901 my father went back to Zara, he met, probably at his grandmother's, this other Nishan.

"He gave me a job," my father writes. "He had a small store. He gave me half of what I earned. He collected lots of worthless things. Tavet Agha (a member of the Gurin family named Vartanian who had migrated to Zara and had befriended my father) said, 'My boy, you have to be careful about the Sherinians. They are liars.'

"My grandmother had a donkey and a cow. She had a place where she kept them to kill for the winter food. He [Sherinian] used to go with the donkey and take wheat and bring back other foodstuffs. Sherinian exchanged this place with my grandmother for a field. The poor woman now had no place to keep the animals."

The record as written by my father is in translation, and thus not too clear, but there was a lawsuit, and Nishan Sherinian won. "He was always very smart in protecting himself," wrote my father.

Soon thereafter, Sherinian made the critical move for the Saints. "He sells everything, my store also, so that we could go to America. He auctioned everything. He was very successful. Everything was sold."

So, this little clan of Sherinians, augmented by the Gagian relative from Gurin and now the Kezerians, Gagosians, and others from Zara, mingle with the Mormon missionaries closely enough that sometime in 1901, Nishan Gagian, together with the other Nishan, Nishan's daughter, Arick, and son Hrant, are baptized in the Kizil Irmak, the river running at the edge of Zara.

Coming to America

The Road to Zion

So, the little Zara colony began gradually to make its way to America and to the mountain country of Zion—Utah. My father noted September 25, 1902 as the date he departed Zara, leaving behind, with a regret he often later told us about, his little grandmother Khatounmar and the relatives of his father.

> It was the fall of the year. We set out in a horse-drawn arabace [carriage], reaching Samsoun in eight days. There were two other families coming to America, one from Sivas, the other Erzerum. We took the packet-boat and in eight or nine days arrived in Marseilles. We stayed two days in Paris and then took a boat from France to America.

Coming from a land where food was not plentiful, Nishan was amazed that food on board ship came as part of the ticket. He remarked that he even had food left to throw overboard to the fish.

When at long last the party reached New York, they found that each had to have twenty dollars to be admitted into the country. He relates:

"The three years I was with Sherinian I had been able to save six

Turkish Lira. He had it. He gave me a $20 gold piece so that I could show it and enter. I paid him back later."

The party then took the train across country, arriving at last at the Union Pacific station in Salt Lake City. How long this journey took, what their impressions were, where they stopped, and what their thoughts and anxieties might have been, I find no record.

My father writes:

> When we arrived we walked four blocks to the office of the Mormon church. They gave us rooms. A few Indians were there, also. They then notified the missionaries who had been in Zara as guests of Sherinian that Zara people had arrived.
>
> The missionary Larson came and took us to his home. It was Thanksgiving Day. He had learned Turkish with Armenian letters. He was a very religious and kind person. He had a few big, giant daughters, one of whom wanted to marry me but I refused.

Faith and Hard Work

These few converts to a new religion and a new country must have been bewildered at the sparsely settled Salt Lake Valley and its great expanse of open space. A new language spoken on the streets and the mélange of new immigrants who had arrived to work in the mines and smelters must have further disoriented them. Perhaps at this point they recalled with misgivings some of the stories they heard back home about making one's way in the New World.

The Mormon publication *Millennial Star* at this time put forth the admonition the missionaries were no doubt expected to use in telling prospective immigrants what to expect.

> These good people have been told time and time again about the life of hardship in the Rocky Mountain West. They were told that Utah and the surrounding states are

comparatively new lands, lying out in the arid region of the American continent; that there is very little rainfall during the summer months, and therefore, without the aid of irrigation the whole land would have been desert; that if they wish trees, they would have to plant them; that if they wish grass, it would have to be sown and then watered all through the hot, dry summer months.

The missionaries were themselves not far removed in time from the pioneers who had traveled by covered wagon or walked with their handcarts across the thousand miles of the Great Plains and many more hundreds of miles over the Rocky Mountains to reach their destination—a place they called Zion, a place no one wanted, so they would be left alone in relative security. Some of these missionaries were direct descendants of these intrepid pioneers and could recall pioneer grandparents or other relatives who had given firsthand accounts of the trek westward. "The Inter-Mountain West," the Millennial Star reported, "is but fifty years old, and all the streets and towns are not yet paved. In the summer there are dusty roads and parched plains; in winter the roads are muddy and the snowdrifts lie deep along the fences. Nature out there is wild and rugged, and the people who dwell there oftimes partake of the wildness and ruggedness of the environment."

If the Zara people heard this warning, it didn't deter them. After all, their own town was not fifty but five hundred years old and still didn't have paved streets. Dust and mud could describe not just their town but most of Turkey. And as for the wildness and ruggedness of the inhabitants, they had just lived through, if they were lucky, some of the wildest times in the memory of this Christian people in the Muslim Ottoman world. Probably what they listened to instead was not the bad but the good.

"The west is full of promise," the Millennial Star continued, "full of opportunity, full of hope, such as the people of the overcrowded countries of Europe do not have. The soil of the West, under the magic touch of the water which is led from the mountains streams through the irrigation canals to the farm lands, is very fertile. There is yet land to be procured … and to those who are not afraid of work there are opportunities." Although this account was addressed mainly to Europeans, especially to people in England, where most of the converts to the Mormon Church were still coming from, it applied equally if not more aptly to these more or less lost souls from the interior of Turkey.

They would have been more responsive, no doubt, to words like these if they heard them: "There is a glory in being the first in a new country. There is inspiration as well as hard work in subduing the desert, in breaking the sod for the first time, in planting the first trees, in building the first rude homes, in making roads, in building bridges, in erecting mills and factories. In doing these things there is a close contact with true life—the life of a creator."

Nishan—my Nishan, I'll call him, for he wasn't my father yet—began slowly to pull away from the other Nishan and to make his own tracks in this New World, this promised land. He got in touch with Missionary Booth, back now from the Turkish Mission. Nishan always spoke kindly of this man, as he did of all the missionaries, for he had been baptized by him and no doubt had confessed to him his loyalty to the new faith.

> Booth took me to his house. He gave me a job. I used to cut wood—did so for a month. I stayed a long time with him. He gave me fourteen dollars.

Then, another important missionary, Hintze, reappeared.

> He wanted me to go to Lakeside. It was winter. I went and worked there. My share from the work was paid. I had stayed for a time with Nishan Sherinian. He wanted $150 for the time I stayed with him. Then I told Hintze and he paid for it with money that belonged to the church.

Nishan Gagian, still a bachelor; May 1907

Naturalization certificate; Nishan Manoug Gagian;
July 18, 1910, Salt Lake City, Utah

The 1910 Arrivals

It is now 1910, some twenty-five years since the first Mormons
had made their way to Zara from the headquarters of the Church's
Turkish Mission in Aleppo, Syria, all within the vast bounds of
the Ottoman Empire. The Armenian communities throughout this
part of Turkey have been ravaged twice during this time by their
neighbors, whose indifference or animosity was acquiesced in or
promoted by the regime and some brigands and outlaws outside the
tenuous hold of the law, which the government in Constantinople
is unable or in some places unwilling to enforce. The missionaries
themselves have been harassed and threatened, their spiritual faith
and physical endurance having been put to the test time and time
again in their determination to carry their message to the far reaches
of this land that spans Europe and Near-Asia.

Some twenty-five of these men over these years have preached
the Bible and the Mormon doctrines. Some have gone out from
their headquarters in Utah more than once, unpaid, unhoused,
venturing out as if on a mapless sea to save souls and bring some
back to Zion. One or two have met their ultimate fate there and
never returned. Their early words of warning to the converts not to
expect that paradise is awaiting them but to promise that faith and
hard work will bring them the rewards not only of this life but of
a celestial hereafter convince a small number of their flock to leave
their ancestral land in search of this better life. Not only will there
be physical hardships recalling those of the pioneers who founded
the Zion of the west but "they should be prepared to endure any
amount of persecution the Lord may see fit to allow their enemies
to inflict upon them on account of their religion. They should be
prepared to find there as bitter enemies to the cause of God as are
to be found in the world."

The picture is not all gloomy, though. By 1884, the year the first
missionaries reach Zara, halfway across the world lies a high plateau

which, once a desert, is now replaced by "fruitful fields, smiling gardens, and happy homes." Utah now contains more than two hundred prosperous communities.

One of these is the town of Murray, seven miles south of the founder's capital of Salt Lake City. Here, in time, we will take up the story of Nishan and Hosanna. But first we must revisit the remaining converts back in Zara for further historical background.

The Kezerian Family

As noted earlier, there had been a rift in the Kezerian family over the influence of the missionaries. Grandfather Gougas had welcomed them. His son, Hovhannes, Hosanna's father, may not have rejected them outright, but he did not become a convert. For reasons unknown, he did not want his children to go to America. They did, though, make some advance preparations for the trip, which may not have escaped the notice of their father, living as they did in very close quarters in their stone house in Zara.

Hosanna had a close relationship with her sister, Miryam, who at the time of Hosanna's departure was married with two children. Whether her husband, Esahag Sherinian, had planned to follow in the footsteps of the elder Nishan and migrate to the United States, there is no record. But Miryam gave Hosanna some mementos from her own hope chest to take with her on this bold journey: a kilim rug that she and her aunt Propion had made during those long winters. Hosanna also packed a two-piece Turkish towel set Miryam's husband, Esahag, had brought from Sivas and given to Hosanna earlier, maybe for a hope chest of her own. She also brought two quilts, one made of wool from the sheep of her grandpa Gougas and one belonging to Nishan. There was also a keepsake piece of embroidery, with edging crocheted by Hosanna, made by her Zara neighbor (and possible relative) Memsar Gagosian (who later married Missionary Woodbury and moved with him to St. George, Utah). There was also a length of checkered woven wool that her mother had made. Was this from a remnant of wool of the sheep stolen by the Turks in the 1895 raid? These few worldly possessions were packed in a trunk and loaded onto a horse-drawn cart.

Accompanying Hosanna on this outward journey were her brother Antranig; his wife, Lucy; and their baby daughter, Nevart; Armenag Kezerian, Hosanna's first cousin; Antranig Gagosian, Hosanna's second cousin; and the latter's family. They left Zara about 1910, arriving in New York and later making their way to Salt Lake Valley. Whether the two Nishans were there to meet them one can presume. They evidently did not gather under the wings of any of the missionaries.

Hosanna left behind in Zara: Grandpa—Gougas
Father—Hovhanes
Mother—Gulvart
Sister—Miryam
Brother—Ezekial, age sixteen
Brother—Mukhetar, age thirteen

Out of the family of nine children, four had already been buried during Hosanna's youth—Perpone, a girl of sixteen, joining the three other little ones, Ashooki, Esahag, and Arshalous, who had died in their infant years.

Also left behind were:

The two little girls, Arshalous (a favorite name) and Lucy, children of Miryam
Esahag, brother-in-law and father of these two girls
Ezekial's wife, Aznig Sherinian, and their boy, Khachig
Propion, Hosanna's aunt by marriage to Krikor
Krikor, Hosanna's fraternal uncle
Agagan Kezerian, a shoemaker whose relationship is not clear

First Years in America

The two Nishans, Arick and Hrant (the children of the elder Nishan), and a few other families, having arrived in America in 1902 and having settled in "Zion," the Mormon country, were gradually making their way in the new and so different world from their homeland. Here the colony they adhered to was not the Armenian one envisioned in earlier years by the missionaries but the larger American territorial colony of the Mormon religion, where they would merge with people from Europe—English, Scandinavian, Swiss, German, and others.

But apparently, they still clung to the hope that they could maintain their ethnic identity. Language alone might have dictated this desire, since there was no such thing as adult classes where English was taught as a second language. Even if there had been, the urgency of making a living, the difficulty of getting around in the spacious valley, and the lack of learning, even in their own tongue, would have been formidable obstacles. Beyond that, though, Armenians had lived in a sea of Muslims for centuries, so with or without the social structure of a colony, they were trying to maintain their old ways while assimilating to the religious and civic requirements of their new land.

Nishan's memoir is scant in detail. He writes that he went to Silver City, still in Utah, but out of the Salt Lake Valley. There he ran into Jesse Knight, a mine owner who gave him a job.

> The two of us (mine workers) worked together. They used to bring up buckets of soil and the horse would pull it up. They would send it down and I would fill it.
>
> One day there was an explosion. It lasted throughout the whole day and the evening. We were buried under boards. Workers came and pulled us out. If they had not done so, we would have been dead. I was hurt—feet and head. My friend was hurt in the shoulder. The good Lord saved us.

At the time a worker was paid a dollar a month for medical care. They sent me to a hospital in Provo, Utah. I stayed there ten months. Jesse Knight gave me $750. He was a good man. I limped for six years.

Nishan's memoir is unclear at this point. He says he went to work at a mine in Eureka, Utah, and worked there four years. He stayed as a guest with a missionary from Provo. He was paid $30 a month.

Jesse Knight was a very rich man and a very good man. I bought shares in the mine and then sold them. I learned the ways and I earned $2,000. Don't let me forget that. It did me a lot of good.

Meanwhile, these few Armenians were looking toward the day when at least some of those left behind would be able to join them.
In Nishan's account, Nishan Sherinian requests $150 for the time he had stayed under his roof. Nishan I, not having this money, goes to Elder Hintze, for whom he had worked and tells him the situation.

Hintze paid for it with the money that belonged to the church. It was with that money he brought four families. He also told me he paid $150 for Hosanna. The relatives came in 1910.

The explanation is not clear; whether it was Nishan's initiative or Elder Hintze's that the invitation went out, the passage for these few new Saints of Zara to get to America was paid for by the work of a predecessor in collaboration with one of the early missionaries who had brought new converts to the church.

Early Life in Utah

Before it was settled by the pioneer church in the mid-nineteenth century, the Salt Lake Valley may have been quite different from the missionaries' description of the rough mountain basin. Other sources have described it as an oasis rather than a parched desert. The valley floor was said to be grassland with flowing creeks and many small springs. In our time, we still used to bring water from an artesian spring down the hill from our place to do laundry and wash our hair. It gushed out of the ground endlessly and was ice cold. If only it had been on our own acres! My mother's cousin Arick had such a small spring right in the basement of her house within the town limits, so by installing a pipe and metal tap, the family had a perpetual rivulet of water, a fine resource for a large family.

An Inland Empire

The valley had, in geologic times, been a great inland sea which, in receding over the eons, had left a base of rich soil needing only water to be productive. Indians from the agricultural Fremont tribe and later the more nomadic Utes had used the wetlands to raise corn and other crops. The pioneers found herds of wild horses in parts of the valley, dissected as it was by a winding river, appropriately called the Jordan. This river was not far from my father's pioneer place. Swampy pastures and little pools filled with cattails bordered the river. Willow trees with their long, feathery tendrils formed green bowers, and occasionally a tall cottonwood gave a mass of shade from the blazing sun. Summers were scorching, just as the missionaries said, but glacial waters cascaded down the canyons the entire season from the snowy mountain peaks, replenishing this precious resource.

The whole valley was agricultural to begin with, but after the discovery of copper and iron ore in the western Oquirrah Range, the building of several smelters in the central valley began to change not only the landscape but the people who lived there. The church leaders were farsighted in laying out an orderly plan of development for the valley, with a grid of wide roads and small settlements, but they seemed not to have realized the potential wealth that lay in those distant hills to the southwest and could not imagine the industrialized towns that emerged. Or perhaps they wanted to keep their "Zion" rural with simple, honest farmers, hard-working, God-fearing, and loyal to their faith.

Conflicts between the mining industry and the farmers resulted in lawsuits over the sulfur emissions from the smoke of the ore furnaces that ruined crops in the vicinity of the smelters. They also forced the smelter owners—"easterners" who took their fortunes out of the west—eventually to erect the tall smokestacks that became valley landmarks, to diffuse the sulfur smoke high in the air, diminishing the toxic contents before they floated to the ground. One of these stacks, at our town of Murray, reached nearly five hundred feet into the sky, but the air on a summer day was still sultry and darkly polluted before the wind would rise from the south and blow it up and out of the valley.

Murray, where a few of the Zara families settled, was the largest town outside of Salt Lake City. With the smelters came workers from every imaginable nationality—Greeks, Slovaks, Italians,

Scandinavians, a scattering of Armenians (not just converts), and others. The original pioneers were mainly from England and set themselves apart as this new foreign element came into the valley. I grew up feeling a little lower than these blonde English and Scandinavian "angels," and when we were asked at elementary school where our parents came from, I disguised my answer by saying "Asia Minor" rather than "Armenia." It would not have mattered anyway, because nobody, including myself, knew where either place was. Turkey was, however, familiar on our geography maps, and when a boy called me a Turk, I was silently mortified, for I had heard my mother from infancy onward speak of "piss Turks" (dirty Turks). She had her reasons, but I didn't know them then.

The town of Murray, a mile high and facing a mountain range another mile into the sky, had about forty-five hundred residents and, with the influx of immigrants, began to have its own identity. Some of it was unsavory, especially in the eyes of the church authorities. The town eventually, according to a history published in 1992 on its one hundredth anniversary, had forty-seven saloons, breweries, gambling establishments, dance halls, and houses of ill repute. The town motto during the 1890s was said by this source to be "If anybody went dry on State Street ... it was his own fault." By the time the Roaring Twenties had passed and the Depression had set in, some of these places were closed, but the coffee houses and pool halls were always there.[3]

What was happening? The pioneer Saints had left persecution against them behind to seek refuge in a place where they could create their communal religious society. They had chosen the valley because they thought no one wanted it and they would be left

---

[3] Data in this paragraph, as well as some of the descriptions in this section of early life in Utah, are from *Between the Cottonwoods: Murray City in Transition* by G. Wesley Johnson and David Schirer. Salt Lake City: Tumpanogos Research Associates. Permission granted by Murray City [Utah] Corporation by email on February 7, 2018.

alone. But it was inexorably becoming part of the great expanse of the United States, no longer a geographically embraceable inland empire, no longer the Zion the missionaries had envisioned a few short decades earlier.

Marriage, "Willy Nilly"

Nishan is now thirty-five years old. At that time if a man lived half a century, he had probably reached or exceeded life expectancy in America. Today he would be a young man, an eligible bachelor, but then he would have been considered middle-aged, if not old. Nishan now has a new country, a new faith, and for those days, a pretty sizable bank account. "Don't let me forget that," as his memoir says. "It did me a lot of good." But he is seriously maimed. And he doesn't have a wife. He had been unlucky in love, but it had not been for not trying.

In Gurin, in his youth, he had mentioned a "flower sister," implying an emotional tie. Then there was Arick, the daughter of the other Nishan, who had refused to marry this "old man." In Zara, he mentions two daughters of his relative the electroplater, Lusig and Sarig. "I wanted to marry Lusig, but I did not succeed. Sarig wanted to marry me, but I did not want her." And then in America, there was one of the missionaries' "giant daughters" who wanted him, but whom he rejected.

So, at last, there is this twenty-four-year-old Hosanna Kezerian from Zara, who chronologically is a woman but who sees herself as, and by experience is, still a girl. But to Nishan, she is a person from his own Armenian background, now also of the same religion, and she is available. The marriage is arranged, possibly by her brother, Antranig, and by which other relatives is not known. She detested one of her aunts, Felor, wife of her maternal uncle Tatos; could it be for that reason?

I grew up hearing my mother say, "They forced me to marry

him." Who "they" were and how the force was applied, whether Nishan knew of or was party to it—none of this did I know then, nor do I now. I never heard my father talk about it. But in his memoir, he hints of it: "Willy-nilly, we were married." He was an honorable and a good man, but did he compromise in this most fateful of life's great decisions? I never judged him, nor did I ever question whether my mother's statement was true. But it must have been, or why would she have repeated it over and over again in the distant years to come?

They lived for a time in Moab, Utah, in that unique Four Corners place, barren of verdure but rich in the earth's underground treasures. But before long, they moved back to the Salt Lake Valley, where the other Saints from Zara were putting down roots and where brother Antranig had settled. Nishan bought four acres "of good land" from the Miller-Calhoun Company. "I told them I had $2,000. They agreed. I paid the money. And on that vacant lot I built a three-room brick house."

It was winter and bitter cold when they moved to the new house, which was heated only by a wood-burning stove in the kitchen. Ruth, their first child, was born April 14, 1913, so all this happened around that year. Being lame from the mine accident, Nishan still worked hard. I am not sure whether he worked in the iron-ore smelter in the town of Murray, where most of the immigrant population was finding work, but he mentions that his pay was $3.50 a day, which was what the smelter paid—good wages but for heavy work.

This I do know: he farmed his land. Just as the missionaries had said, if he wanted trees, he would have to plant them. And he did—apples, plums, apricots, cherries, and lots of pear trees. How well I remember those pear trees. Some, close to ninety years later, were still standing, their stark, twisted branches bravely bearing a few golden pears when I saw them last.

*Nishan and Hosanna, in their
new home in Murray, Utah, c. 1912*

Hosanna, with Baby Ruth, c. 1914

*Isabel (the author) in front of "the little red brick house"
at 242 West Forty-Eighth South, Murray, Utah*

War and the Zara Saints

Now comes that fateful year of 1914 and the start of World War I in August. There is a curious silence about it in Nishan's memoir. The war lasted four years, so it is odd that he hardly mentions it. For that, Hosanna's oral history sparsely fills in the gap, but it leaves a question of why the blank in Nishan's account. For Armenians of the twentieth century, World War I has one meaning, which the world by now knows about well enough: deportation and death. The events of that time are still being played out in countries today, even after most of the people who were alive then and were part of that history are gone. Some of those histories are still being written.

There had been some communication between the emigrant Saints and those they left behind in Zara in the years between 1902, when my father arrived in Utah, and 1910, when my mother came in the company of her brother, his wife Lucy (from the Sherinian clan), their child Nevart, and my mother's cousin Armenag. My mother or her brother had corresponded with Esahag, their brother-in-law, and as the war started, there was a letter from him saying the town of Zara was surrounded by soldiers, and this would be his last letter. What further message it contained is lost. After that, there is silence. But in time, there are reports, relayed over the years by people who heard, saw, or lived through experiences like those of her family. What she knew and when she knew it I cannot piece together, but certainly by late 1915, reports had come out of Turkey of the great mass deportation of Armenians from all over that country to the deserts of Mesopotamia, the Iraq of later times.

My father too had left behind relatives whose whereabouts were lost. In fact, every one of the Zara people in America was suffering the same anxiety and distress. In time, it seems one could not meet an Armenian anywhere who did not have a relative lost in that great forced migration. After the troubles of 1895, followed by those of 1909–1910, the missionaries pulled out of Zara, and the mission itself disbanded when the war started. It was not until well after the war ended and the whole political map of the Turkish Empire was redrawn that enough stability was established for the missionaries to return. That would not be until 1920.

Meanwhile, back in Utah, Nishan and Hosanna were settled in their little red brick house at 242 West Forty-Eighth South, on their four acres, in the town of Murray. Two more children, Lily (Shoshan), and Isabel (Vartanush), arrived in 1916 and 1919.

"For eight years I had a good family life, I had a good home," Nishan wrote. These were the years up until 1919 or 1920. But did Hosanna have a good life? She had lost her parents, her brothers, her sister, and her extended family. She was in an alien country where she did not speak the language. Her brother, who had brought her there, had moved away. Her cousin Armenag who came with her had joined the Sherinian family, whose unfriendliness to Nishan had rubbed off on her.

The missionaries' tracts had warned that there would be not only physical hardships in the emigrants' new home of Zion but enemies, both outside and within, who would be there to test them. "He who expects to find Zion must take Zion with him, for Zion, remember, is the pure in heart, and that purity of heart must exist in the individual wherever he is on the face of the earth. The booking of passage to Utah will not give it to those who do not have it."

For Hosanna, words like these, if indeed she heard them, may have had little meaning, given her loss and her loneliness. Nishan's mining accident had left him permanently maimed. The good family life which he remembered years later may not have been shared by his wife, and he may not have understood the reasons why.

The missionaries have disappeared from the local scene after the early years, when they shepherded their converts by giving employment and spiritual sustenance. In their place is the established church, divided up into "wards" or sections of the community. Families live in different wards, depending on their physical locality.

Nishan and Hosanna live in the Marray Second Ward west of the railroad tracks. The other Nishan, his daughter Arick, now married to Hosanna's cousin Armenag, and other new arrivals live in the First Ward, east of the tracks. The other Nishan's son Hrant is now a medical student at the university in Salt Lake City.

Hosanna's brother Antranig has moved to the mining town of Price, Utah, where he takes up the family vocation of sheep-raising, which he had worked at with his father and grandfather in Zara. Hosanna's uncle Tatos, brother of her father, settles in Provo, Utah. Some of the people from her mother's side, who had also come to Zion, settle in Salt Lake City. Rather than a gathering, there is dispersal, so what could have been a little Armenian colony of Saints from Zara is soon immersed into the large sea of the Saints of Zion. Alienation and isolation begin. So, slowly, does Americanization.

6

The Family Breaks Up

My first memories are of looking out across the lush alfalfa fields to the splendor of the mountains on that good land my father had bought. It is a picture of a happy child. I came to these parents' lives on a cold January day in 1919 in that red brick house my father had built in the heart of Salt Lake Valley. Two girls, Ruth and Lily, preceded me; we are a united family. But, as the poet says, "Nothing gold can stay."

My mother cries all the time. That I remember more than anything. When anyone comes knocking at our door—the milkman, a traveler, gypsies (of which there are many)—she tells them the Turks have killed all her family: "my mother, my father, my sister, my brothers, everyone." These callers do not understand and give her no comfort. The years from 1915–1916 onward are filled with bitterness for her, and Nishan is powerless and perhaps stoic in the face of this inexplicable tragedy.

"But one day one comes knocking who does give comfort— Anush," writes my father:

> It was the devil who came to ruin us, to destroy our house—a bad person, Anush Egnoian. He came and turned my wife's mind and caused me much harm. Missionary

Hintze, who lived not far from Murray, came on hearing of the trouble. He examined our condition. He understood Hosanna's mind was really not very good. He said she was mentally disturbed. One day Nishan Sherinian and his wife also came, but Hosanna had been carried away under Anush's influence. They asked how much money there was. Hosanna said, "I think he has $1,000."

"Well, $500 let him give you and $500 for him. The house and one acre for you."

My father had said that he had "learned the ways" of the New World sufficiently to earn money buying stock. Now it was Hosanna who was learning the ways, this time in the courts. And how greatly, in time, to her grief.

Hosanna agreed to what was proposed but she had a lawyer. From her share we gave $50 to him so he would not bring suit. He wrote down the conditions of the separation. I gave the $500. We separated. They put me out. Ruth 5, Shoshan 2, Isabel 1, and Samuel 6 months old. Four little lambs left crying. I left in 1920 for Fresno, California.

He doesn't say, but I can imagine he shed a few tears himself as the train rumbled by his fields at West Forty-Eighth South.

My mother is now free from the marriage she did not want. In Armenian society in Zara, this could never have happened. Nor would it have happened among the convert Saints, had she been able, as the missionaries advised, to carry Zion with her in her heart. Years later, my mother would say, "God bless America. You can be free here," or words to that effect. She also said if her own father had come with her, things would have been different. How could she have known the price of this freedom?

This Anush—or John as he was called ever after—had some negatives but also some pluses to his credit. Besides being Armenian, he was about Hosanna's age, well built, good-looking, and unattached.

He had a job or had come to Utah to get a job in the ore smelter, which had drawn a large section of the valley population to the town of Murray. When he and Hosanna met, he was living as a boarder in a house close by Hosanna and Nishan's house. Later, he lived in a small smelter company house about two miles away. My mother would take us small children to visit him. We would play outside in the dusty yard while she was inside with him. It was a long wait and a long walk.

They did not marry right away.

We had a cow that my mother took care of. In summer, there was fruit. She baked flatbread, she dried vegetables for the winter, and she learned to bottle fruit. So somehow, we lived and had a house and food. I remember the day John came to live with us. My mother baked lemon custard pies—not at all a part of our usual Armenian food. Someone taught her that—maybe the lady who lived next door in the house just past the tall cottonwood trees.

We all slept in the same room, which was taken up mainly with beds. There was a brass bed my father had bought, which "they" slept in. In winter, the blankets my mother had made from the wool of her grandpa's Zara sheep kept us warm.

John Egnoian, c. 1920

Hosanna Kezerian, c. 1920

Nishan's Exile and Return

In Fresno, where my father went after the breakup, there were a lot of Armenians, but it was worlds apart from the community of Saints Nishan had left behind. In the 1920s, California was still pioneer country. Land was cheap. Vast open territories, expanses of citrus groves and vineyards, small rural settlements, and a stream of people from all over the country converged. The "Okies," who aroused the animosity of the earlier settlers and landowners, were to come later. Nishan found work in a mining compound and tried to nurse himself back to emotional health.

"They gave me an outdoor job in a quarry. It was a nice place," he wrote in recollection. In time, he made friends among the Armenians.

> Those days a woman named Macroui came from a place twenty miles from Fresno—Sutters, near Hanford. She was from Dikranakert [Armenia]. She had a daughter, also Macroui, and a boy named Peter. She praised highly

the Fresno suburb she came from and said the land there was $50 an acre. People told me, "Whatever Macroui says, do." So I went one day. Pete had a house. He took us lots of places with his mother. I acted foolish. It's too bad I didn't marry. I don't know whether it was from God's will or not. I left and went away to get a job building a railroad in the mountains. It was cold and beautiful."

Meanwhile, two years having gone by, Nishan's old nemesis, the other Nishan, now once again on a mission for the church, along with Armenag Tavoian, another of the Zara converts, find their way from the Salt Lake Valley to where Nishan is working. They say to him, "Your children have no shoes. They are hungry; they have no clothes. Go to them."

As is well known, a Mormon, to be entirely true to the faith, should give up his or her worldly endeavors for two years and go, as Christ commanded, to preach the gospel. So now Nishan responds to these convert missionaries, his Zara compatriots, and returns to Utah. He goes to the red brick house, where "the little lambs were so happy to see me." He does not say so, but the happiness was certainly not shared by Hosanna and her new mate.

My Three Parents: Early Sorrow

John, though healthy looking, already had a lung disease caused by the flue dust in the big smelter furnaces. He coughed at night, a deep, persistent cough that brought up mucus. A coffee can under the bed contained it.

John was an Armenian, but he was not a Saint. He had come to America with his father sometime after the 1915 calamity. They were from a small village near Erzerum, about a hundred miles east of Zara and about that distance from the Russian border. That eastern province had been the scene of battles from ancient times onward.

Persians had vanquished Armenian armies there in the days when Armenia was ruled by kings and had an empire. One of those kings had been taken captive by the Romans, whose expanses had spread to the very foot of the Mountains of Ararat. The Seljuk Turks slashed their way into western Asia in the eleventh century by beating the Armenians at the battle of Manzigert, written about by military historians in the centuries to come. Russia and Turkey had contested each other throughout the nineteenth century. Kars, Ardahan, and Erzerum had seen their share of savage warfare between these two watchful and wary powers—Christian and Muslim.

People who came from those eastern places had ties on both sides of this border between Russia and Turkey. Part of ancient Armenia lay within Russia and part within Turkey. Western missionaries had penetrated to Van, the border city, where they had been attacked, along with the Armenian inhabitants, in 1915. But, as far as I can tell, the Mormons from the "Turkish mission" in Aleppo had not reached that far, so whether there were converts from Erzerum in Utah I do not know, but John had no contact with the Church. His father had come to America and returned, so we were told, when World War I and the Armenian troubles began, in order to join the "Armenian Legion" to fight against the Turks. John, young though he still was, had left behind a wife and two boys and they were presumed to have been lost in the deportations. He made no secret of his contempt for the Turks. Nor did he hide his sympathy for the Russians and eventually for the Bolsheviks. As far as I know, he didn't read Russian, but he did read newspapers put out by the Armenian revolutionary "Dashnags." Formally uneducated as he no doubt was, he was a working man with a cause.

Those years of the Roaring Twenties may not have been bad ones for my mother and John. I was with my mother those early years after the war, and my first language was hers. I, and all of us children, spoke Armenian first and then English from playmates and eventually school. But there was no real Armenian community where we could go to school, as Hebrew children do, and learn to read and write the mother tongue. My father did not speak to us in Armenian. My mother slowly acclimated herself to American ways but wanted to hang on to her Armenian language and family memories, while my father seemed to leave all that behind and cling mainly to the new religion.

There were two boys now, Sam and Art, and John used to take them to workers' meetings in town. Somewhere I would hear talk of Communism, of the workers' flag, of Russia. When the war came, he could be openly sympathetic to the Soviet Union, the new American ally. He even believed in the Soviet Socialist Republic of Armenia, being as it was not many kilometers over the border from his old town of Erzerum. But even though his true allegiance may have been elsewhere, he was a true American working man when it came to performance on the job, and during the war, he was recognized as such for dedicating himself to working long hours and double shifts for the war effort.

Hosanna, at our Murray place, c. 1940s

Having settled in a place of his own on Fifty-Third South, Nishan would go to his remaining acres next to the red brick house, now Hosanna's, with John also living there. The situation was tense, as his field was next door to the red brick house, and the three parties couldn't avoid each other. My father writes:

> I had another quarrel with John. He wanted to make a fence. I had with me Sam Kavranjian. Hosanna came and quarreled. There was a fight with Sam K. John grabbed

him by the throat and was going to choke him. A shovel was in his hand. I hit him. He turned to me and knocked me down. Sam saved me.

The police arrived, and the case went to court. Nishan had to pay dearly—$150 to his lawyer and $450 to John's lawyer. "John's doctor told me I would lose the suit because I had hit him with an iron." The case was settled in court. "Finally, we won," Nishan said.

I myself was too young or perhaps not a witness to this actual scene, but the consequences remained long after it was over and pervaded the lives of all parties concerned. My mother seemed to derive from it a new reason to fuel her dislike of my father, and she would not speak to him whenever he appeared to take care of his land next door. The boys, Sam and Art, and I were drafted in turn to work in the field, thinning sugar beets. My mother didn't like my being friendly and solicitous with my father when I saw him hour after hour without food or water, working in the field, sometimes late into the night when his turn came to irrigate.

It was a contentious household. As I grew older, I would walk the miles between the two, now three parents' places, tears of anger covering my face as I stumbled along the railroad tracks. Nishan and John eventually mellowed and would exchange greetings when they encountered each other on the road or in the town, but Hosanna never bent in her anathema toward Nishan, the first husband, and in time toward John, the second.

Nishan with one of his beloved pear trees, c. 1945

Valley Stories

The first pioneer house my father found after his return from California was a wooden two-room structure on Fifty-Third South, more rural and rugged than the solid brick house on a good road where my mother and John now lived. I must have been five or six when I went to my father's place. Ruth was there too and maybe Lily. This house was so ill-constructed that in the winter, the wind blew right through it. As insulation, my father covered the inside walls with oilcloth in a blue-and-white pattern of squares. I had a little game of half-closing my eyes to make the squares recede or move forward at night by the dime light of the kerosene lamp.

A Pioneering Life

My father's house was surrounded by a field where, that first spring, he planted a garden—corn, melons, potatoes, and root vegetables—and he managed that way to provide us with a pretty good existence. He couldn't work at the smelter because of his injury from the mining accident. Winter was especially austere, but it was also beautiful. The pond beyond the field was frozen for months, and from the house I could see children ice-skating, with outdoor log fires glowing in the blue evening light. Sparse as it was, there was a feeling of home in my father's place.

There I met my first childhood friend, Lois Swenson, a girl my own age, though one I looked up to as an older sister. Her house was up the hill, with a stone front. A profusion of flowers surrounded it in summer. The Swensons were a large family, all handsome, Nordic-looking people. They were members of the church. Mr. Swenson worked in the smelter. How they were able to live on a worker's salary was due in good part to their dedication to thrift and to growing their own food. Mrs. Swenson became like a mother to me and my sisters. She sewed lovely dresses for us. One she made was a lavender organdy with a ruffled skirt trimmed with delicate white lace. That one was for Lily, who was white-skinned and pretty, while I was brown as a berry and in my own eyes unsightly. I longed for that dress but felt it was too elegant for me, but it implanted in me a desire for such things.

We walked to Bonnyview School, about two miles. Winter snowdrifts were no excuse for staying home. There was a man who made his living selling doughnuts. He carried them in a box on his back to the store near the school. When we saw him on the road, Lois and I and the others would corner him and say, "Just one, please," and he would always give us each one. They were still warm and sugar-glazed and the most inconceivably wonderful of treats.

At the elementary school, we were given soup and crackers at lunchtime. Mrs. Smith, the school janitor's wife, would bring a large, steaming pot of it from her house at the end of the school grounds to the soup room and there, seated on benches at long tables, we would savor its herbal aroma and enticing warmth. That was sometimes the only hot meal we would have that day.

On Sundays, Lois and I would go to Sunday school together. Church was a fundamental part of our lives, and it encompassed most of our social activities. My father would always be there, sitting up on a podium with the other elder Saints. The Mutual Improvement

Association for youth allowed even dancing on special occasions, though I was too young and too clumsy for that. I would stop at the Swensons' on the way home from church, and they would invite me for Sunday dinner—a pot roast, mashed potatoes and rich gravy, a bowl of crispy vegetables, and heavenly homemade ice cream with cake for dessert. Usually I would pretend I wasn't hungry, though my stomach was rumbling with emptiness, and Lois would insist and force me to the table. It was a sort of ritual. They were a fine family.

There was a field next to the Swensons' house where they grew alfalfa for their livestock. In winter it turned into yellow stubble and then into a soft white bed when the heavy snow came. Spring was late, with the elevation of five thousand feet, and March was probably the coldest time of year, the wind from the north blowing through the black, icy branches of the poplars at the edge of the fields. If by chance there was a warmer day, Lois and I would be out playing with our dolls.

My father had rented his house for five dollars a month, so he looked for a place to buy. He found one a distance away, a true pioneer cottage on the edge of the railroad tracks. It was equally spare but more solidly built, with heavy plaster walls and a thick pine floor. But it lacked heat, water, plumbing, and everything else that makes a house. It was as primitive as those places he had left behind in his town of Gurin. But it was not in hostile country.

Even though it was only a mile from the first house, the move uprooted us, especially me, completely. I had to make new friends, and in leaving the bonds of friendship with Lois, I also lost the embrace of the entire Swenson family. It seemed we were descending in the world, and the location practically on the railroad berm was visible proof of that. The new neighbors were part of the church community, it is true, but they didn't seem as friendly as the members we had left behind.

The railroad tracks were our transportation route by foot because we had no car. The double track that passed our house fanned out like a delta around the ore sampling mill, with a network of switches, signals, and lighted semaphores where the road crossed over the tracks, a treacherous place which, through the many future years, often appeared in my dreams. There had been a fatal accident there with a whole family demolished when a speeding train hit their touring car one night. So, we were wary enough when we walked between, and often on, the tracks. The railroad was also our timekeeper, since we knew by heart the times the trains would pass, all day long and into the late-evening hours.

My father and all the families living along the tracks were like scavengers, keeping the railroad levees clean by gathering up the replaced railroad ties and hauling them home for firewood and other uses. My father dragged enough of them home to build a chicken coop. His structure was reminiscent in its crude design of the kind of building I saw much later in Turkey, with dark horizontal timbers and white stone spacers in between. Oiled swabs of lubricating cotton and wool would fall out or be replaced in metal jackets above the wheels of the rail cars, and these would be gathered up to start fires in the stove that heated our house. My father also used them to oil the pine floor of the main room of our house, coating it in time with a thick, hard layer of grease, protecting our bare feet from the slivers of the rough wood but also leaving the bottoms of our feet black.

This house of ours had no running water but a shallow, brackish well and a creaky iron pump to draw up what scant supply there was. We used the water to wash dishes, but it was undrinkable, so we carried drinking water from our neighbors, the Youngbergs, over the levee. That was my chore, just as it had been my mother's in her home in Zara when she was a child. My father did the laundry by hauling the bedding, his temple garments (a union suit with a special insignia cut out in the area over the heart), and other household items in a little red wagon along the railroad tracks about a mile north past the sampling mill to where the tracks crossed the Jordan River. There he would hand wash everything in the cold flowing stream, wring out the still-gray things, and haul them home to hang on a wire clothesline, so the laundry was not done with any regularity until spring came.

It was a way of life for a lonely man. But I don't think in his daily chores my father was unhappy. Depressed, perhaps, at times if he contemplated what might have been, but in summer, at least he had his garden, his small flock of chickens, which he seemed to regard as pets, his kitchen, which emitted a savory aroma from the round robin of stews that were perpetually simmering on his wood-burning stove, and his Bible. That, and mostly that, he read every day, posting in

Murray Second Ward (Mormon), where Nishan (and the author) attended services every Sunday.

Armenian script on the brown-painted wooden walls of the kitchen the prophecies and warnings, and the words of hope and uplift, that he gleaned from this well-worn book. The messages were mere reminders to him of the Christian faith, for he knew all the essentials by heart. He never failed to pass these messages on to me on a daily

West Fifty-Third South, facing east. The road to Murray from Nishan's house on Anderson Avenue.

basis, deaf though I became in my youthful arrogance to his admonitions.

There was, though, a sadness about him. At least I felt it when I came to visit him as the years went by and when I was older and moved to my mother's place to be nearer school and also to help her. He limped, so John and others referred to him, as people did in those days, by his infirmity as "topal," (the lame one), and if he had walked a lot on a particular day, he would sit down with a resigned sigh of pain. Those times I felt a deep compassion for him.

Winter in the Valley

In the absence of a regular job, people had to rely on their own inventiveness to get by in those days. Men were on the move everywhere, in search of a place that might be better than the one they had left behind. Living close to the railroad, we would see the boxcars filled with these vagabonds with nothing but a fragile hope to sustain them. We always waved at them, and they waved back. Sometimes a stray on foot would come to our house to ask for food, and my father never turned anyone away. A stranger might be Christ himself, he would say. The valley brought forth its abundance in summer, but by September, the high elevations of the eastern range had already turned white, and by Thanksgiving, frost and often snow had descended into the valley.

During the long ensuing months of winter, my father was housebound, but he was not idle. His small brood of chickens forced him outdoors to feed them. On Sundays, he went to church, rain or shine. He laid in supplies of flour, lard, dried beans, nuts, and the hard pate he had learned to make way back in the days, now receding in memory, of his youth in Gurin. He filled his cellar with apples and insulated the small windows with straw. So, he was self-sufficient in an austere way. He read the Bible, and as I said, wrote out in Islamic fashion its verses all over the kitchen walls. And he took up knitting.

One day, a heavy wooden box arrived from Bangor, Maine. It contained a disassembled knitting machine, together with skeins of brightly colored yarn and an illustrated manual of instructions, which were too complicated for me to understand, far less to explain to him. Somehow, he got the thing set up on three long iron legs holding up a cylinder and placed it at the foot of his bed, with light coming from an adjacent window. There he would sit for hours, threading the wool onto long steel needles inside this cylinder and hand-turning the arm that made the whole thing work. Once he learned the basics, he was able to make socks, stocking caps, and mittens, some in rainbow colors. When I would visit him after school on my way to my mother's, I would find him humming away at this machine, a wood fire glowing from the cast-iron stove nearby. If it happened, perhaps by my interrupting him, that a needle would not close and would drop a stitch, he would say, "An-be-dawn," which is equivalent to "darn it"—the strongest epithet he ever used—and peer into the cylinder to rethread the steel spike. So passed the winters of his ebbing life.

At my mother's house life was not so cheerful. When the harder times hit the valley and the smelter laid workers off, John, my stepfather, left at least for a time. He was going to Saint Louis, he said. Why there, we never knew. In the summer, my mother got work at Camp Murray, a concrete-block motel not far from her place. It was owned by Mr. Bee. He was a tall, blondish man who wore gold-rimmed glasses and carried a gold watch on a chain tucked into his vest pocket, which gave him an air of distinction. He spent his days behind the grocery counter in his small shop at the entrance to Camp Murray and lived in one of the motel rooms, which was also his office. Mother cleaned the rooms and made the beds, but there wasn't much to do after the summer season. Mr. Bee let a few people, mostly homeless single men, stay in the rooms even when they couldn't pay. Chief White Eagle, a Ute Indian, would come to the camp dressed in his great feathered headdress and grayish-white buffalo-skin garments studded with turquoise and colored beads. He and his entourage of women and a few children would attract small crowds and bring in a few customers to Mr. Bee's establishment.

Mother earned a very small intermittent salary, augmented for Sam and Art, my two younger brothers, with root beer and potato chips. This was a poor lunch for growing boys, but they loved it and begged for it on days when Mr. Bee was not around to give out this largesse. That first winter of hard times, Mother could not heat the red-brick house, even though we lived mostly in the kitchen and one bedroom, so she moved a mattress and her wool blankets to Mr. Bee's motel room, where she and the boys slept on the concrete floor. It was dark and cold but warmer than the frozen interior of our house.

One winter afternoon lodged in my mind through the many years long after we had left the valley. I was living at my father's place a few miles distant but would stop at Mr. Bee's to see my mother on my way home from school. She had entered a world of darkness, of mental depression and hopelessness, which had blocked me out. Art was only about five years old and at her side all the time. Sam, three years older, had already become something of a breadwinner, bringing home heads of lettuce that had fallen out of the boxcars carrying food on the railroad or wandering through the neighborhood in search of trinkets.

That afternoon, only Mother and Art were there in the motel room. I was with my school friend from this other home of mine on Anderson Avenue, and I was wishing I were alone, so that I wouldn't have a witness to the destitute picture there at the camp. As we left slogging through the slushy snow, I turned back and saw the forlorn face of my little brother through the frosty window pane, waving his tiny hand at me, with a shadowy outline of my mother's dark head behind him. My heart seemed to burst with sadness. "What's the matter?" my friend said as we walked on, but I couldn't answer and turned away from her to hide my tears.

The Red Truck

Not being able to work in the smelter, and equally unable to farm his fields, my father sought other ways to make a living. He was always occupied with something, and he never, even through the Depression, asked for or accepted anything he didn't work for. The federal government's New Deal welfare program for the unemployed and indigent did not count him on its rolls. Even the welfare program of the church did not include him. Quite the contrary, he lived on what he could make from his self-employment, and meager as it was, he still paid his church tithe. "We must give something to the poor," he would say and would take a basket of eggs from his henhouse or a pair of socks he had knitted to some person who was more in need than he.

One year, he decided to rent a peach orchard up in the foothills of Draper in the south of the valley. To do this, he bought an old red Dodge truck with sturdy wire mesh panels on the sides where he could carry equipment and in time, with hope, the peach harvest. The orchard was vast, sixty acres; it was up on high ground, where there was a grand vista of the farms in the valley below. We lived close enough to it to work there by day and return in the evening, though sometimes we camped overnight at the edge of the peach trees, where the irrigation ditches intersected. Tall cottonwoods, willows, and sumac grew along these watery corridors, which were fringed with mint and wildflowers. The valley was laced with green from this water system.

My brother Sam and I were old enough to help with spraying the trees in early May and with the irrigation through the summer. We would set out in the cool dawn and reach the orchard before the oppressive heat bore down on the valley. At lunchtime, we found a cove in a rock outcropping to have goat cheese, bread, and yogurt, and later in the summer, watermelon, which my father placed in an eddy of the icy stream flowing down from the canyon. Near the stream, there was a green sward of ground edged by aspens and maple trees, which may have been an old pioneer homestead. A few wild rose bushes emitted a delicate fragrance when a rare breeze stirred.

I loved my father, but as I got into my teen years, with the influence of peers overshadowing my home life, I dishonored him time and again down in the valley when my friends and I passed him on the street and I pretended not to know him when asked if that old, ragged man was my father. But up here close to heaven on the plateau with the acres of pink peach blossoms framing the iridescent blue-green valley below, I felt close to him and a deep sympathy and sorrow for his suffering.

In midsummer, my father hired a young man named Koni Houpiana to help with the coming peach harvest. He came from Hawaii, where the church had a mission, and was himself a new member of our ward. Koni knew a lot—where to get the bushel baskets to carry the peaches, how to pack them with leaves and straw so the peaches wouldn't get bruised, and most importantly, how to drive the truck and relieve my father of the long journey on the road south to sell the crop. Koni drove with us in the red truck each day and worked relentlessly, getting to the higher branches of trees, carefully picking the fruit and directing us to pack it.

Koni was short and bulging with muscle; he had shiny, black, straight hair and a round face dominated by a large mouth, always stretched open with a smile showing enormous square teeth. He looked a little weird. I liked him but not my brother's teasing about him. My father seemed to be watching whenever he and I were working together.

Toward mid-August, the peaches were ripening to a rosy glow but still firm in their fuzzy skins. My brother and I wanted to go on the trek south to sell the peaches, but my father thought it would be too hard for us to endure the long drive, and anyway there was no room for us in the truck, now loaded down with basket upon basket of peaches already giving off their pungent fragrance.

Koni and my father left at once, hoping to make good time in the cool hours of the evening, on the venture to southern Utah. Disappointment dogged their sales trip. People wanted this fine fruit from the north, where the best peaches were grown, but they had no money to pay for it. They tried to barter but for things we didn't need or want. Some success greeted the two peddlers further south, where tourists even then had discovered Zion and other parks, but when the time came in early September to turn back, the two peddlers still had half a truckload of peaches. They stopped along the route and gave away the still-edible fruit. Some had rotted from the heat and was thrown out in the trenches along or beyond the road. I guess my father hoped the pits would germinate the next spring into fine little trees.

There came a day in September when I went to town with my father. The trip had been hard on the red truck, which was moving along in a heavy jolt, and he was looking for a repair shop. That was when it broke down in the middle of Main Street, in front of city hall. The back end of the car had collapsed. A policeman came and instructed my father to move the car. When that proved impossible, he wrote up a ticket, which to my amazement and embarrassment my father tore up right in his face. I was afraid he would be taken to jail, but the policeman gave him a lecture and let him off with another ticket, increasing the fine. The truck had a broken axle and would have cost too much to repair, so somehow my father got it towed home to his lean-to garage, where it was propped up on concrete blocks, having earned its rest.

Late that autumn, my father became seriously ill. Whether it was from some infection he had picked up on the trip, loss of strength from the work at the peach orchard, or perhaps a general weariness of life's struggle I didn't know. He took to bed and couldn't get up for days. The sick room itself could have contributed to his illness, dark as it was, with flaking kalsomine from the walls and a general gloom and sadness everywhere. He probably lay there wondering how he would pay the taxes on his fields and how he would get us through the winter.

Three men came every evening from the priesthood of our

church, elders who performed the laying on of hands, anointing him and praying for his recovery. Each afternoon when I returned from school, I brought in buckets of cold water and made cold compresses for his forehead. He ate hardly at all, and for a time, it seemed he would not recover. No doctor came, but the elders appeared each evening, faithful in their prayers. I prayed silently along with them, promising the Almighty that if he would spare my father's life, I would be a good Saint forever after.

At last the fever consumed itself, and he slowly recovered, thin and gently frail for a long time to come. He never gained enough strength to return to the heavier work of farming, but he spent a lot of time after that summer working on the red truck, lying on the ground and peering into its insides. It gave him employment and hope for the future, but he never got it to run again. I was only now entering my teens, and there would be ample opportunity in the years ahead to beseech the Almighty for my trespasses, but while I was still in my father's house, the red truck was planted there in its resting place as a reminder of the best reprieve I had already been given.

Community Spirit

On one side of the pioneer house lived the B family, with origins in Germany, and of the Lutheran persuasion. I don't know what brought them to Utah and to Salt Lake Valley. Mr. B had a preciseness about him and dressed like a pastor. He wore white shirts with a high collar, and he was always dressed in black. I never saw him in work clothes, and I don't know just what he did to make a living. He played the violin and gave music lessons, but I doubt that he could have made enough money from that to feed his many children.

His wife worked at the canning factory. I remember seeing her walking along the railroad tracks, swollen in pregnancy, mumbling and gesturing on her way to the canning factory. There were children of every age and with odd names. Some were my playmates.

When Mrs. B was not at the factory, she spent many hours doing the laundry and baking bread. They had one of those wringer washers that I used to crank for her, watching the clothes come through paper thin and all of a uniform gray color. Water for the wash was heated on the wood stove in a massive copper boiler. The clothesline ran the length of the yard, and in winter the men's underwear, or union suits, would freeze on the line and hang there for days like human forms out of which the bodies had escaped.

Mr. B built a miniature wooden church that decorated their front yard. When I say front, I have to explain that the front of their house, and my father's as well, faced the eastern berm of the railroad tracks, so the houses could not be approached from that side, which in effect became the back of the houses, the front being the west side, sloping down to the levee and the willow swamps. Once later I remember being on the train and seeing that landmark of a tiny church as the train sped by.

I assumed the Bs were Mormons, but I never saw them in church. Some neighbors on the other side of my father's cottage spoke disparaging words against them, words the church severely admonished against. One of my favorite hymns went like this:

Angry words, oh let them never
From the lips unbridled slip.
Love one another,
Thus said the Savior....

They were words my father lived by.

The Bs, with all their faults—noisiness, clannishness, to name a couple—were good to my father. Mrs. B always, and embarrassing to me, brought him a plate at Thanksgiving; the boys gave him rides to town; and the family generally kept watch over his little place. Still, they didn't attend church, so it made me wonder whether the B family was of a different religious affiliation from ours.

"Milk Comes Frozen Home in Pail"

In the time when I lived with my father, young though I was, I had some chores. The milkman didn't come out to deliver as far as Anderson Avenue, so it was my duty to carry supplies home from one of our neighbors about half a mile away. Their name was Anderson, and they were no doubt the original settlers of this area. Their farm had gradually shrunk as the town limits spread to outlying areas. They were Nordic people—Swedish, I think—and spoke with a good-natured lilt. Their two-story blue-and-white farmhouse sat solidly behind a curve in the road, with a view of a sloping pasture along one side of it where their milk cows grazed and left in their tracks innumerable steaming pancakes that hardened when the winter frosts came. Such droppings were dried, stacked, and used as fuel back in Zara, but here they were ploughed into the sod in spring as fertilizer.

I would take a two-quart bottle to Mrs. Anderson's kitchen door, where I was invited in to wait while she went into her pantry to bring out a large pail of milk from which, with an aluminum ladle, she filled my bottle and tightly closed it. I would sit quietly during this interval, looking around at every object in her clean, orderly kitchen, hoping to prolong the minutes ticking away on the wall clock. Everything here was peaceful, clean, and sparkling, even the linoleum floor, and the warm air had the pleasant aroma of baking bread. If I happened to arrive at the right time, Mrs. Anderson would give me a thick slice, heavily topped with her creamy butter. Sometimes I would fall into a misty reverie and wonder what it would be like to be adopted and live there with the Andersons. But I would feel a sharp stab of guilt in my heart and would return to the reality of getting on home before dark with the milk and to my father, who would be waiting for me at his door.

One day, my father drove his red truck, the same one before it eventually broke down and was mothballed in his garage, into the Andersons' gravel driveway, thinking to buy some straw for his garden. He used straw as a mulch to keep down the weeds in his little patch of corn, where blue morning glories would climb up the cornstalks and overwhelm the whole garden if unchecked. My father hadn't had the truck very long and didn't really know how to handle such a powerful machine. He tried to turn around in the narrow part of the driveway adjacent to the house and stepped on the gas when he intended to brake. The resulting crash left a huge hole in the side of the Andersons' house. I was there and was terrified that not only my father but Mrs. Anderson inside the house had been mortally hurt and also that my father would go to jail. It turned out, though, that he was able to walk away from the crash and Mrs. Anderson was unharmed, but the repairs would cost all the money we had. I saved my tears until the bitter winds of winter, when I would be carrying home the milk not in a bottle, which might break if I fell on the ice, but in an uncovered pail, frozen into crystals before I could reach home.

The Leopard Coat

Once in a very great while, my father would take me to Salt Lake City, and we would go window-shopping at ZCMI, the big dry-goods store there that had been founded by the early pioneers. It was wonderful to see all the beautiful clothes and luxurious things for the big houses in town. Everything was far too expensive for us, but just to look was an excursion in itself. My clothes were handed down from my sisters, and theirs for a time were made by my friend Lois's mother while we lived on Fifty-Third South. If my father had earned some money from his land, we could also order things from the Sears catalog, the encyclopedia of American material ingenuity. My father had ordered a set of wooden chairs from Sears when we moved to Anderson Avenue. They had to be assembled and were intended to be painted, but instead they remained a weathered-looking gray.

One autumn when the new catalog had arrived, I spent hours

looking at the section on clothing, as I had nothing warm to wear with the cold weather approaching. A leopard coat caught my attention. It was not leopard, of course, but described as a velvety brown velour with creamy light spots all over. I became fixated on this coat and finally showed the illustration to my father. I never came right out and asked him for it, or for anything really, but I longed for it. He didn't have the enormous sum of eleven dollars it would cost, so nothing more was said about it.

The weather had already turned cold. One day, I went with my father to the slag dump at the base of the smelter, where he had been working on his own to recover shards of ore that had escaped the furnace and still had veins running through them that could be processed into copper. No one objected if a person took the time to search through the piles of slag to recover these pieces of ore and take them to the sampling mill. A pile that would fill a small cart could be hitched to the back of a car or truck, weighed at the mill, and sold there for a few dollars. My father worked at this for quite a few days until the first snow came, and he sold several carts to the mill.

One day a few weeks later, with the winter winds whipping about our little house, a package came. It was from Sears, and I couldn't contain my curiosity and excitement. What could it be? Maybe it had come to us by mistake. My father was not home when it arrived, so I waited until evening, trying to imagine its contents. At last, when the moment of revelation came, I saw the velvety spotted fur. No animal could have been softer. I wore that coat for years until I had far outgrown it. What took shape in my memory most of all, though, was not the coat but the picture of my father bending over the rocky slag in search of threads of copper ore shining in the winter sun.

The Pear Trees

When spring came again, and with John no longer there, my father would come to my mother's house, where I now lived most of the time, to take care of the fruit trees. He had given up trying to farm the acres, being unable to get any help with the sugar beet crop he had planted a season or two before and turning the fields into alfalfa or renting them out. Taking care of trees was not as onerous for him as irrigating the beet fields all night in the torrid summer or topping the beets, some weighing ten pounds or more, with machetes in the muddy fields of October, limping to his home miles away after a day's or a night's work. I wasn't much good to him in that kind of work.

But taking care of the trees was different, and there he asked for my help; I gave it without the murmur that might be expected from a thirteen-year-old. He had a sprayer on wheels, but it wasn't the kind we have today where you push a button and a fine spray mist spumes forth. My job instead was to pump the sprayer to get this mist. We did this in spring when the pear blossoms had reached their fullness so that the sulfuric chemical could nip the larvae in the bud. Then we did it again in midsummer to coat the green young pears, to keep little predators from boring into the maturing fruit. That first spray in late April or early May could be completely undone by a late spring snow. In Utah that could happen as late as Decoration Day, as it was then called, at the end of May.

We had glorious springs, and at our place with the peach, apricot, cherry, plum, and pear trees putting on their spring garments, it was a paradise to walk under the fragrant blossoms at dawn or in the fading light of evening, with the majesty of the mountains in the background. It didn't happen every year, or we would have had no crops at all, but when those late snows came, they could freeze the delicate flowers in their tiny green pods, and even though the snow would be gone the next day or two, the frail white blossoms had turned brown, and the crop was ruined. Such is the fate of the world, which finds Eden only to lose it.

But we persevered and had faith that this year, as my father might say, the Lord would spare us and spring would march on bravely to summer. I liked being a help to my father because he needed me. He didn't benefit from this work, just did it for us. My mother would stay in the house when he was there. Did she still bear her old animus toward him when she looked out the window and saw this old, crippled man? Was it bitterness that filled her heart? Or did she possibly feel guilty about what she had done? How should I know? It was not for me to say.

By August, those pears had ripened to a pale, golden color, with flecks of soft green still in their firm flesh. No insects had penetrated their armor, and they were as perfect as a pear can be. Is it any won-

Nishan and his pears

der that artists the world over like to paint them? We lived on a busy road, and as people would drive by our house in the evening, seeing the bushels of fruit lined up in our front yard, my mother and I would be there, she in her housedress and I in my overalls, ready to realize the profits of the summer's work. I may say that although my mother didn't participate in the spring work, she had come out of her depression through the summer and had, with my help, gathered in the fruit.

For a bushel of pears, we got three US silver dollars; there has never been a more beautiful coin minted in the world. Nor had a better bargain ever been made between a buyer and a seller.

Family Life

There were now five children among these three parents of mine— or to put it more accurately in my way of thinking then, my two separated parents and then John. Ruth and Lily were from the first marriage, Sam and Art from the second, and I in the middle, with loyalties divided between Hosanna and Nishan, who had separated about the time I arrived because of the interloper John, a person who, in my mind, loomed large when he was around but one best to be avoided if possible, even though his labor bought the bread we ate.

My sister Ruth had a determined, high-tempered personality. There was an animosity between her and my mother. Whether it was based in their opposite natures or developed in the new family situation, I could not know, but it came out into the open with tearful tantrums and screaming on both sides. I was a small, silent, and neutral observer, which in time became a trait of my personality. Lily was all sunshine—giving, generous, and pretty—and unarmed for the battles of life that awaited her. Sam got the brunt of the dissension, not adequately loved, it seemed, by any of these parents, but a fine-looking boy. And finally there was Art, the baby, exceptionally bright even in infancy, and loved by everyone.

How were these people to fare among two households, where there was only one able-bodied worker, whose religion was atheism;

a crippled but meek and righteous Christian man who had dedicated himself to the Saints who had saved him; and a woman like a pilgrim stranded on the high seas, an emotional shipwreck? The setting is a rural religious community undergoing a transformation, with an influx of immigration and industrialization in the midst of hard times. The three adults will make their way as best they can. The five children will go their separate ways, the first generation venturing out into twentieth-[h]century America with hardly a compass among them.

My story started out about the Saints of Zara and the missionaries, but one by one, they are falling away. My mother's brother, who came with her to America, has moved away to coal-mining and sheep-raising country; it's only in the next valley, but we hardly ever see him again. The Sherinians, my father's relatives, are aloof, and one of them, Hrant the doctor, who came to America with my father, has moved to a lucrative practice in Los Angeles, although he was needed in our town. The Kezerians, my mother's relatives and my cousins, live not far away but are near-strangers now, even though one of them is my classmate in school.

Hosanna's brother Antranig with his three children (Nervart, Louella, and Albert) and her daughter, Lily, second left,) who went to live with them in Price, Utah, after her marriage to John.

So, it seems that the Saints in my world have dwindled down to one, my father. In the early days when I was with him, none of the Zara people or the missionaries was there, but our life was circumscribed all the same by our church. One Christmas is an example. The church always put on a pageant, for which we began to rehearse right after Thanksgiving. Two young people were Mary and Joseph, small children were angels and cherubs, and the baby was a doll or sometimes a real baby that always managed to cry at the wrong times. Dressed in a sheepskin throw, with a twisted wooden walking stick and with his limp, my father looked authentic as one of the three wise men. It was a safe, friendly world where people addressed each other as Brother and Sister and where we were all included in a figurative and real family enclosure.

This was one of my worlds. The other was my mother's house, where there was no joy. With her divorce from my father, bold and unusual in a community where marriage was the norm, Mother was soon treated as an outcast, a fallen woman, by some of the townspeople. Once she told me to go to the canning factory, the only place where jobs could be found, to ask for employment for her, but the manager said, "No, not that woman."

As I grew older, I sensed her isolation and unhappiness. As life with John became more and more contentious, there came a point when Ruth, the oldest but still only in her teens, put the case to my mother: either John must leave or she would. It was the beginning of the second family breakup and the first step in the new emigration—this time from our high valley to another foreign land—California.

"Though Our Hearts Are Broken, Yet We Shall Be Glad"

Ruth's ultimatum to my mother got her nowhere, so she left, first to Uncle Antranig's, who had two daughters of his own, Louella and Nevert, and a new, foreign wife. They lived in Price, Utah, which, as I said, was sheep-raising and coal-mining country. For a time, I lost the thread of Ruth's life because she stayed with these relatives only a few months in a harsh rural setting, and then, like everyone it seemed, headed to California, the land of sunshine and promise. Lily, three years younger, soon also left the inhospitable home of my mother, where John was now more a visitor than a resident. It was the depths of the Depression, in the early 1930s, and people were migrating like birds in search of work. So, the two girls, still in their tender teens, had gone forth guilelessly to find their destiny.

I was now left as the oldest child, with two isolated parents, three miles apart but incommunicado. Two quarrelsome boys now seemed to be my wards, but with my mother alienated not just from the Saints of Zara but the entire church community, I had little influence on these two brothers. Sometimes they walked with me to my father's house. He treated them well, but I think he was something of a curiosity, a relic, to them. They made up a game of the two fathers meeting and exchanging imagined conversation in character with their opposite personalities. Children made up their own amusements at that time. Soon, though, we had the radio and movies.

My mother and I were not close, but I became her helper. In summer, she gradually grew out of her depression and began bottling fruit from the trees surrounding her house, and I worked with her. By summer's end, the cellar shelves would be full of large bottles of apricots, peaches, pears, and tomatoes, and there would also be a supply of dried beans and dried apples. She began to develop a little self-reliance, and that lifted her morale. It was uneven, though. In winter, I would come home from school to find her lying on a bed she had devised: a board held up by two chairs and covered with pieces of blanket, edging up near the wood stove in the kitchen. Sometimes she would have made macaroni soup, sometimes nothing.

It was not cheerful, but what did I know? I had my schoolwork to do and my chores, both there and at my father's place. Such were the days of my youth. I had everything because I had a life of the imagination. But my parents had long ago lost their youth, and they had lost a lot more. They had lost each other; they had lost the possibility of holding the family they had created together; they had lost the remotest chance of prosperity; but most of all, they had lost what they had come to America to find: their faith in themselves and in their dreams.

My father's impoverished way of living, the hopelessness of it, caused me passing moods of melancholy. One of the last times in summer that I walked with him up on the railroad tracks toward town, we rested at our usual stopping place, about halfway along the route. There was a sort of cove near the tracks on one side of the sampling mill, where a wooden box that controlled the flow of water in the irrigation ditch paralleled the tracks. Sometimes on a scorching summer day, we would sit there in the shade of the surrounding willow trees, take off our shoes, and dip our feet into the arctic waters of the ditch that had flowed down from the still-snowy canyons. On this occasion, my father mentioned my two sisters, who had now been away from home for some years and were heard from only at irregular intervals. His thoughts wandered, and he said, "My heart is broke."

So, content though he had learned to be with the hour thereof, his sorrow at that moment covered him like a shroud.

Intimations of Elysia

Although branches of the family had broken off and made their way to California, they—being my two sisters, Ruth and Lily—didn't forget us. Young as they were, they had found employment—Ruth taking care of a household and Lily as a waitress. They were not only supporting themselves but every now and then sending small tokens of their good fortune home.

Sometimes a letter would come to us from Lily with a silver dime wrapped in tissue between its folds. A dime could buy pound of hamburger. It could also take me and the youngest of my brothers to the movies on Friday nights and inject untold excitement into our lives. The old cowboy movies and adventure serials were subjects of endless conversation and material for storytelling to less-fortunate children who hadn't the means to go with us to the Iris Theater in town. Neither Hosanna nor Nishan ever accompanied us, except on one occasion—was it 1936? —when my mother, brothers, and I went to Salt Lake City to see *Gone with the Wind*. My mother still had a strain of romance in her, as I could tell from the way she sighed at the sight of Rhett Butler.

Besides the coins in letters, my sisters sent other harbingers of California. Lily's job as a waitress put her at a crossroads with customers who were truck drivers. The great web of interstate highways across America was still in the future, but well-traveled roads north and south across Utah, as well as the east-west continental railways, had made Salt Lake City a transportation hub and Murray a tributary branch of it all. With her sunny personality, Lily persuaded one or more of these truck drivers who befriended her to drop off a crate of oranges to us at my mother's place. The oranges with their ever-lasting fragrance, were each wrapped in tissue, and we made a crate last from Christmas all through the snows of winter, sometimes up until St. Valentine's Day, when, if luck was with us, another crate would arrive. I cannot describe the joy this gift of abundance from the Elysian fields of California brought us. I can only hope that I carried some of it with me on my winter walks to see my father.

A Night Visitor

My mother's health continued to be poor, and after the winter at Mr. Bee's Camp Murray, my sisters sent the bus fare for her to go to California, as a new cold season became unbearable for her. And so she went, taking little Art with her and leaving me and Sam behind. I was still in high school and Sam a few years behind me. I can't recall how we managed, but when the weather began to thaw a little, by late February or early March, an event jogs my memory.

One very blustery night, with windows and doors rattling and the mulberry tree in front of the house lashing its branches against the walls, I heard a loud knock at the front door. Who could it be? I wasn't afraid, but I was immobilized, so I didn't answer. The knock persisted and became a heavy pounding. Still, I did not answer.

The autumn before, we had had a visit from "Tatos," my mother's fraternal uncle, who had come to America with one of the group of Zara Saints. He had married—was it also into the Sherinian family? I only knew that his wife was "Felor," and I had the impression my mother harbored animus toward this lady, who had had a hand in arranging her marriage with my father. They had settled in Provo,

Tatos Kezerian
Mother's uncle, brother
of her father.

in the next county to the south of us, and there Tatos had gone into sheep-raising, as had my mother's brother Antranig in the valley east of us. Tatos had come to visit us once. He was very distraught, and the story was that he had come to Salt Lake to pay three thousand dollars to a man who was to deliver to him a herd of sheep in Provo, that he had turned over the money but had never received the sheep, and that the deceiver had simply disappeared.

After that, this poor man, having lost his life savings, was so disoriented that he was committed to the insane asylum, for which Provo was then noted. He had escaped but had returned or been forced back. But somehow, he got free again, and it was he who was there at midnight in a blizzard, pounding at our door. I don't have a picture of my grandfather, who was one of the brothers of this man, Tatos, but there must have been a resemblance. Anyway, why would it matter? At what moment I realized who it was, I am not sure. I like to think it was after he left, but I'm afraid it was while he was out there at the door, freezing and lost, that I knew. Was it caution or was it an inborn indifference as I peered out the window to see this outcast man stumbling away into the night? I never saw him again, but I cannot forget that he was there.

California Stories

In the thirty years since Nishan had worked in the lumber camps of the central highlands, the world had changed as greatly in that once-pioneer land as it had in the Salt Lake Valley. By the 1950s, when I first started my winter journeys to take him there, Los Angeles County was already a chain of urban corridors that became the matrix of the huge population center it is today. But even with the great influx of people from all over the country and the world, citrus groves, fruit orchards, and vineyards still richly embraced the clusters of small houses and townships. Out toward-the-sea tall grasses still grew in pastureland, and manicured Japanese farms supplied the city residents with fresh produce daily. The misty breezes from the sea still washed the air and kept it fresh. Smog was an unknown word.

Over the years, the California years, I went there over and over again, so as not to sever my ties with these parents and this family of mine. Many winters I would take time from my work to go to Utah to take my father to California, where he could escape the frozen Utah mountains. Often it was at Christmas that I would go. He would have to leave his little brood of chickens to the care of the neighbors, and I would prod him along, since my time was short. We would take the train to Los Angeles, leaving the chill and stillness of the valley behind. The trip was all downhill, and within twenty-four hours, we would be coming in view of the great cirque of the Los Angeles Valley, warm and sunny with the fragrance of citrus groves and lush farm country going all the way down to the sea. I would leave my father there with one or the other of my sisters for the winter. He would encounter my mother, who was living with Lily, or later in a place of her own, but I don't think they had much, if anything, to say to each other. They were strangers now, as I believe they had always been.

When spring came, my father would return to his home in Murray, to his church, and to his friends in Zion. That is where he always wanted to be. Once, when he had been away for months and I saw him again, he said, "I want to go home, to put my feet in the snow again."

In 1960, I had a letter from him, written in his phonetic English, saying he was losing his vision and darkness was overtaking his life. This letter disturbed me greatly. Why could I not take care of this poor, lonely man, this person who had suffered so much in life, in his fading years? It seemed all I could do, as I had done before, was go to him and take him to my sisters in California. I had delayed that year, and it was March before I could make the trip. I was shocked to see him when I got to his house. He looked dark and hollow, like the haunting picture he had sent me. The years of insular living, spiritual though they may have been, had usurped his vitality, his gladness to be alive.

At that time, the miraculous discovery of restoring vision by replacing the clouded lens of a cataract was largely unknown. The method extant left the patient with scarcely any vision after removal of the cataract. This was one of the accumulating afflictions my father was heir to. He had no faith in doctors and had lived well into his eighties without their interference. But loss of vision was too serious to delay, so he agreed to a cataract operation.

Hrant, along with Arick and their father, the "other Nishan," had been part of the party of Zara Saints coming to America in 1902. My father was some years older than Hrant, and for reasons I could never fathom, there had been a stream of antagonistic feelings between these Sherinian relatives of my father toward him. Still, my father, for his part, had long since forgiven any trespasses and had enough faith in Hrant to seek him out for this operation.

My sisters were involved in their own problems, so it was left to me to take him from Inglewood, where they lived, to the doctor's offices. Dr. Sherinian—Hrant—was receptive enough. He showed me a large formaldehyde-filled jar of lenses he had removed from his many patients' eyes. I think he was a good doctor, but I was quite fearful my father might end up blind, so I prayed a lot. I don't know whether the doctor was still a member of the church—I think he was—but when it came time to pay, his fee seemed exorbitant, considering my father's circumstances. During those years of my working life, I had regularly sent my father money, and instead of spending it, he had carefully saved most of it, which now went to pay for this operation. I suppose it went as well as could be expected, but without the lens, the light hurt the raw exposure of the cornea. My father devised for himself a pair of aviator-style dark glasses and felt his way around precariously. After that experience, I could never feel warmth for this remnant of Zion in the California wilderness.

The Fig Orchard

In those years after the war, it fell to my lot, as I said, to travel to the valley to rescue my father before the deep onset of winter and take him to my sisters in California. At first it was to Lily's place, where he would stay till early spring, when he could travel back alone by bus in time to plant his garden and resume his accustomed life among his brother Saints. Later, when Lily's illnesses prevented her from offering refuge, Ruth became the winter caregiver.

Lily's hilltop house had a deep garden that sloped off steeply at one end to vacant land which, like all expendable terrain in Southern California, eventually became part of a freeway. The slope was too sharp to grow anything but trees, so my father slowly turned it into a small orchard of fig trees with a few lemons, plums, and oranges scattered around its edges. He would spend the entire day there, turning the sod, weeding, pruning dead wood, and cleaning debris. He made a little bower there for himself where he could rest in the shade and contemplate the passing world below. At midday he would climb a stone path up to the flat garden of flowers; take a spare lunch of bread, cheese, olives, and water from the house; and return to his bower for an afternoon of quiet work. In the evening, he would come in, wash himself, and eat a hearty dinner that Lily prepared for him.

There were two growing children in the household, Michael and Rona, so he had the satisfaction of being a grandfather for a few years. Dependent as he was on others for everything, sharing his space with others, he seemed all the same able to find peace in a vortex of movement all around him. I always felt unhappy leaving him there because it seemed I was shifting a burden onto people who were not as able as I might have been to provide care, but in those years there never seemed to be an alternative.

Fate has its own inscrutable logic. This interlude ended when Mike, Lily's son, finished high school. He had found a Mormon girl who was going off to Utah to the Brigham Young University in Provo, in the county in the south adjacent to Salt Lake. Following this girl, Mike enrolled there that autumn. He had never lived in a winter climate and had no experience driving mountain roads. My cousin Nephi, Arick's oldest son, had become an orthopedic doctor with a practice in Provo. I wrote him a letter introducing Mike and asking for his good offices as a mentor. Mike was there scarcely a month when he was consumed in an automobile fire on an icy curve of a mountain road one Sunday. I wonder if Nephi was one of the doctors in attendance at the hospital where he died.

After this devastating blow, Lily was no longer able to provide the winter refuge for my father. It may have been that a year or two went by before he could go again, and this time it was Ruth who provided a place for him.

Quest for Lost Souls

Unlike Salt Lake, where the Zara Saints had formed the corps of people from Armenia, California, from an earlier time, around the 1880s, had attracted many Armenian immigrants and later refugees. Many had settled in the farmlands in the north around Fresno, but also from the World War I dispersal, numbers had come to the Los Angeles area. My sisters had encountered some of these refugees and their children in the area where they lived and had made friends on our parents' separate accounts to give them a chance to speak their own language again and perchance to run into someone from the old country, distant in time though that now was.

Hosanna found these old-country people more receptive than her Zara relations in Utah, where she had become an outcast after the divorce from Nishan. At least that is the way it looked to me. She began going to the Armenian church picnics and other social gatherings, often taking with her Art, her youngest, who poked fun at their affairs.

"Onoonut inch eh?" (What's your name?)

"Annoshanoorian" or

"Muatsanazian" or

"Loosagorsagian."

These were not actually names, but Art would add several syllables to the already long surnames that are common among Armenians, to make people laugh. But there was in these antics an element of rejection or derision, deliberate or unintentional, toward the ancient past. Hosanna indulged him as the favored child he was, but in truth, that was a reflection of how some of us were beginning to feel about our first-generation status.

My father did not make a connection with these Armenians. They were of an old religion, backward in his eyes and unenlightened in their souls. Instead, he was forever on a quest to find people from the home place of his youth—Gurin—where he had spent those early years with his maternal grandmother and where, but for God's grace he never forgot, he might have died so young. He did find some relatives of people from Gurin, but his quest never led him to anyone who might have known him there.

One day, an old woman came visiting to my sister's house. It seems she came to see my mother and to exchange talk of the past with her. It happened during one of my visits there. This lady was terribly bent over and ancient in appearance, though she was not beyond seventy. She wore a thick shawl that seemed to weigh and bend her down even further. The conversation became animated, and she removed the shawl to reveal a very deep scar, the result of a heavy blow to the back of her neck. I was standing at her side and could understand most of what she was saying, but she took my hand and placed it in this deep wound, as if to convince me of the actual truth of her words. "A Turkish soldier hit me with his sword," she said. "On the road to the desert in the south." It was frightening to see and to feel—a head nearly severed from its body and yet the person able to survive.

I thought about this lady afterward, with the picture of her bent frame and the awful wound in my mind. Had fate—had God—preserved her, here in California so far away from her homeland, to be a living witness to that terrible time so that no one could say, as Turkish governments repeatedly did, that it never happened?

Nishan—The Road Home

As he had at Lily's place, my father, when he was taken in winter to live with Ruth, made the best of the circumstances he found himself in. Ruth was precise and careful in everything she did. She had a small house that she had added to by building a garage apartment to rent out and eventually expanded her large yard to accommodate another apartment for my father. It was a very small space, but it had a kitchen and a washroom, so they both had their privacy. She had planted a variety of fruit trees, and my father made it his job to take care of this yard, which he swept clean of leaves every day. Ruth did her best to care for him, but their lives were separate. I had the impression my father led a lonely life there.

He knew no one on the street, and he was not close to his church. This street, once a mere country road, was underneath the path of the airplanes as they descended in preparation for landing at the Los Angeles airport, barely a mile or two away. The airport had expanded vastly, and the traffic into it had become so heavy that in the early 1960s, it seemed planes were landing every few minutes. They flew so low that the vibrations shook the houses along their path, and the engine noises seemed to be right on top of one's head. Thus was transformed what had not many years earlier been farmland into a polluted megalopolis.

My father must have found this contrast with the open spaces and clean air of his home in the high desert disconcerting. That and perhaps his homesickness prompted him by spring to want to return to his valley. Once when I was there with him, we chanced to see on the street one of the Youngberg boys who had been his neighbors back home. I turned away, but my father went up to him and embraced him with unrestrained emotion, as if a messenger had come from the distant land of home.

The last time I visited him at Ruth's place, he said, though winter was approaching, that he wanted to go home. He had somehow found some Mormon missionaries and had told them of his plight, of his desire to get back to the mountains, to his cottage, to his garden, to his chickens, and to his own life. He had arranged a meeting place with the missionaries, had packed his single suitcase, and was walking out the gate when my sister arrived home and interrupted his plan. That was when she called me as the alternative to his going home where, with that world soon frozen, he could not manage alone. Before he joined me, however, a journey of my own intervened.

In Search of Things Past

This is the story of the Saints of Zara, but I am also writing about a person growing up in a world entirely different from that of parents, people known only by the reminiscences of their immigrant past. Years and years go by this way, and the gulf between me and my parents widens. Almost everything is receding—the home I was born into, the town I grew up in, the religion that brought my parents to America; all is slipping away from me as I, in my turn, migrate to a new place, a new world, and a new life. But I can't forget this family I leave behind, so over the years, as I said, I travel long distances over and over again in order not to lose touch with them.

During this time, I want neither to forget about the Armenians nor to dwell on them either. It becomes a question of proportion. World War II produced the horror of the Holocaust, and in those alleged words of Hitler, "After all, who remembers the Armenians?" I don't consciously set out to know more, but I am becoming gradually a reader of history, and this leads me to find obscure books in various libraries. It is only in the last thirty years or so that first-generation American-Armenian students and others have begun serious historical studies of the fate of Armenians in Turkey during World War I.

Anatolian Journey

It is now 1962, and I am about to embark on a trip to Turkey. I am to accompany my architect husband, who has a job with an agency of the US government to survey the school system in Turkey. I am not part of the official party, reason enough for me to keep a low profile, but also because of the tense relationship with the Soviet Union, with Turkey in a pivotal geographic position as our ally, added reason for circumspection.

Here I think there may be an opportunity for me to learn something about what happened to my mother's family. All those she left behind in Zara have never been heard from since 1915. It is assumed they were lost in those events, instigated by the government in Constantinople and carried out by Turks. I go armed only with that knowledge and a sketchy picture of Zara and people being driven from their homes on a long march to a desert in the south. Of my father's town in Gurin, I have a shadowy image of green, of water, a church, and his story about being saved in a rock canyon.

There are other things I didn't know then. I didn't know of the American ambassador Henry Morgenthau's book about what had happened in Turkey during that great war. I didn't know about the "Young Turk" regime that had deposed the sultan, sided with the Germans in the Great War, and condemned the Armenians to their fate. I didn't know that many American missionaries had left eyewitness accounts of their own tribulations as the Ottoman Empire was breaking up. I had no point of reference of where to start or what to look for in searching for my lost relatives.

My Search Starts in Ankara

From the moment the dimming lights of the airport appear through the haze of the summer twilight, I feel that I am entering a world at odds with all I have ever known. Although it is the land of my ancestors, it is alien to me. I step foot on its soil with a sense of trepidation. What I am looking for and what I will find are a dark void in the mind. Our base is Ankara, the capital. Before we set out to travel by car across Turkey, we go to an official farewell reception in the Kavaklidere Hills above Ankara. I feel uneasy, as if I am an intruder and don't belong there. I don't know who is leaving, but the refrain from "Auld Lang Syne," "We'll take a cup of kindness yet," stays with me. Tears unaccountably cloud my vision. Perhaps that is all I am looking for—a cup of kindness—and all I will find.

As we had a few days in Ankara before starting out on our journey, I thought I should lose no time and start my search at once. The "Grey Wolf" seemed a likely place. I had heard talk of him at that farewell reception, so with unaccustomed boldness, I found this author of the book by that title about Araturk—Mustafa Kemal—who, after World War I and the defeat of Turkey alongside Germany, had made the revolution that founded the new Turkish state—Father of the Turks. He, the author, seems to be quietly living in a dark garret in the city. It is hot, and I feel gritty after a walk up dusty stairs, where he receives me rather stiffly. I ask straight out whether he can help me trace my Armenian mother's family. He immediately closes off the conversation by saying he is married to a Turkish lady and cannot help. "There are Armenians in Istanbul. Maybe they can help you."

But I'm not in Istanbul, I silently protest. "Aren't there any Armenians in Ankara?" He leads me to the door. I feel puzzled and also downhearted at this first step in my search.

I got back to our hotel room just as the sun was setting. The grayish-purple haze from the distant hills was like a soft descending cloud over the city. I began to recall the names I had learned from my mother of her family. Now, for the first time, I felt they were my family too. What would life have been like in this strange country at the time when they had been alive? Not here in this smoky city, but in that little town of Zara. What did my grandparents look like?

What did they wear? What did they eat? Were they kind to each other? Even the questions I asked myself might not be relevant to their lives, I thought. I repeated the question to myself: *aren't there any Armenians here?*

That evening, I find one at dinner. She is a small, gray-haired lady who is a servant at the home of our American host. She has that Armenian look that I can easily identify. When she leaves the room after serving us at the table, our host refers to her as his Armenian housekeeper. She seems deferential, quiet, lost, just the way I feel. I wish I could talk to her, but of course I do not. She reminds me of my mother, and I wonder if she is my relative, maybe a distant cousin.

The next day, we set out early on our long journey across the country in the summer dust and rising heat—two architects (Y–Bey is Turkish, the other my husband), the driver, and myself curled up in a corner of the back seat of the car. I feel like an oversized piece of luggage. That is good, I think. I will recede into the background and just observe and absorb everything.

We go through countless towns and villages, stopping at every schoolhouse that can be found, the architects talking to local officials and villagers and arguing with each other about roof spans, building materials, alternative structures, and the like. I read the guidebook as we pass through towns along the Aegean and Mediterranean coasts, studded with Greek and Roman ruins, remains of crusader castles, Seljuk cities, Christian hideaways carved in the rocks of mountains, archaeological digs in the Hittite country. Everyone has been here and all have left their mark.

In the south, we skirt Diarbakr and its ruins. Y-Bey looks blank when I cite my guidebook about an ancient Armenian dynasty there whose ruler was taken prisoner by the Romans and sent off to Egypt in the time when Cleopatra held sway across this world. Y-Bey had a disconcerting way of throwing his head back and saying, "Yok," as if to say "yes" but meaning "No" in the Turkish tradition. Then he volunteers the remark that the "Ermeni"—Armenians—were bad, "traitors." I have no idea what he means, but from that point on, I resolve to wear my invisible armor.

Gurin: My Father's Town

Our route took us from the south, from the scorching cotton fields of Gaziaintep—the Aintep of the Mormon missionaries of which I am only faintly aware at this point—up through the Taurus Mountains, and reaching Gurin, the first place I recognize from my Armenian legacy. It is just as my father described it—a green sward surrounded by chalky hills, with a lush spring of icy water gushing into the river that runs through the town. My husband has been asking questions about the makeup of the school populations—Greeks, Armenians, Kurds—and Y-Bey always replies, "Yok."

As we walk around the town of Gurin, I see a boy, hurt in some way, with big, dark eyes and that indefinable Armenian look about him, sitting in the dust against a high wall. Other boys are pelting him with rocks. He looks at me as if begging for help. I protest a little but walk on. The wall he is against, it turns out, is the side of an abandoned church. Inside are the charred ruins of a once-elegant small chapel, now filled with debris. This was my father's church, I say to myself, and step away from the others to touch the blackened stones.

Above the town and surrounding it are the hills pockmarked with cave openings. These must be the caves my father wrote about—one of them, the place where, but for God's grace he would always say, he might have been impaled by the Turkish swordsman in 1895. I am helpless as far as my search goes here. I wish now as I walk about the town that my parents had taught me Turkish. I would love to ask a passerby if he knows where the Armenians went, but I don't dare with Y-Bey close by. I wonder if he has ever knowingly met an Armenian.

Scene of Gurin from one of the caves above the town, 1962

We didn't linger in Gurin but headed north for Sivas, the provincial capital, passing through Kurdish country. Later, back home, I find out that Ataturk's policy of "Turkey for the Turks" was able to finish the work of the Young Turks, who had dispatched the Armenian population and had driven out the Greeks. But Ataturk could not rid

Ruins of a church interior in Gurin, 1962

Turkey of the Kurds, if that was indeed what he ultimately meant by "Turkey for the Turks." Kurds were very much in evidence on this road to Sivas. We could see the women and children, handsome people in their colorful clothes, all along the way. With late afternoon approaching, their silhouettes stood out against the sky as they threshed grain on a turning wheel, the golden husks swirling up as a cloud in the crisp evening air. They must not have changed much through the centuries, but now, unlike the time my father wrote about, they had been disarmed as roving bandits and could not ravage the villages, sometimes with approval, disavowed though it was, of the sultan in Constantinople.

As we neared Sivas toward dusk, we could hear at a distance the clanking of metalwork. This would be the town where my father had worked as an itinerant electroplater. When we got into the city, we found a quarter where the artisans made copper utensils of the kind described in my father's reminiscences. I had heard my mother say Sivas was an Armenian town. Here, then, I would find Armenians. But how? I was at a loss. We found out when we got to our hotel why travel to the east was discouraged. The building was a wooden structure that had long since seen its best days. It was filthy and equipped with an ancient, disgusting unisex type of toilet. Cholera and typhus were frequent visitors here. Our driver got violently sick, but he said he would rather die than go to a Turkish hospital. Within a short time, the hotel manager came by with the kaimakam—the mayor—and an officer in military uniform.

There were few foreign visitors here, and the kaimakam said he welcomed them all personally. He introduced us to the officer, a handsome, well-structured man with an engaging smile. He spoke excellent English and was with the Eastern Region army command. He had trained, he said, in the United States. He asked what our business was and offered his help. As it was Friday, Y-Bey decided to leave us for the weekend. My husband was now also off duty, so it seemed fortuitous that the major had appeared. I wanted to be free, to go forth on my own, but it seemed to me that the major was there not only to host but to observe our movements. His manners were impeccable, but I felt certain he was an intelligence officer and all we said and did would be reported somewhere. Those were cold war days, and the Russian shadow loomed over Turkey from the east. My husband brushed aside my reservations when we were alone and said he would take charge.

At dinner with the major, who was invariably neat and in uniform, my husband said I wanted to find what happened to my Armenian family from Zara. The major's expression clouded. "Ermeni." He nodded. That, I thought, meant negative. But he said he would arrange for a new driver to take us there—it was forty miles to the east—and we could see what we might find.

The heat, dirt, and primitive facilities, together with my anxiety, made for a sleepless night. We assembled at the hotel restaurant in the early morning and made our way out with the new driver. At that time, nearly all the cars in Turkey were American, and this man went crazy behind all that power. He pushed the gas pedal to the floor and gave a wild yell as we roared off, but the major soon took command and got the situation under control, though not before the driver sideswiped one of those magnificent, huge silvery sheepdogs we encountered on the road, along with a herd of sheep, their bells tinkling forlornly after we passed.

Zara at Last

The town square was crowded. Slabs of meat were hanging in the market stalls, with vast colonies of flies feasting on them. The major hurried us by. We walked onto a better street, where the balconies of wooden houses overhung the narrow lanes. These were old, imposing structures from an era long gone. Now it seemed people bulged out of every entryway and window, attesting to the population explosion in Eastern Turkey I had heard about. After half an hour's walk, we arrived at a high wooden gate and entered without formality. The kaimakam asked a few questions of the man who appeared and then left us, but the major stayed. Here, at last, I had found my Armenians.

They were a sparse family—two young girls, a boy of about ten, the father, and an old man. My first impression was that the girls looked like my Kezerian cousins back home—light-skinned, with straight dark hair, and those big eyes that sparkled like wet diamonds. They took us to an upstairs room—square, very scant, with rug cushions on benches all around and uncluttered wooden walls and floor. The major turned to me and said, "Proceed. Ask whatever questions you like."

As I knew no Turkish, I tried out what Armenian I could remember. But somehow, these Armenians spoke differently, and it was hard for us to understand each other, so after a few halting efforts, we had to resort to the major to translate from Turkish. I gave my mother's family name and those of her brothers and sister. I turned to the old man. "Where are they? What happened to them?"

At first, he said nothing, looking at the major, not at me. The major repeated my question. "Oh," he finally said. "That was fifty years ago. How do you expect me to remember what happened then, when I can't remember what I had for breakfast this morning?" The major laughed.

I smiled and touched the old man's hand. "But where did they go? Can't you remember at all?"

He turned to me with a pointing gesture. "They went in that direction, toward Divrigi." He spoke as though they had just left.

"But," I hesitated, "why did you stay behind?"

"I am a shoemaker. They left me here to make shoes."

At that moment, I felt helpless. *This man must be full of memories, but this is all he will say.* He seemed tired and not wanting to talk anymore, and by now, the girls had come to invite us to a meal in the adjacent room. We sat at a long table, and they served barley soup and good bread, but I could not eat with pleasure. Around the room were shiny copper pots on shelves. It was an orderly, clean household.

It seemed a hopeless journey. Then we went into the courtyard with the father. He limped. "They call me 'Topal' [lame]. I was hurt as a boy. We ask nothing from you," he said gently. I felt ashamed, seeing their poverty compared to us. "We are getting along pretty well, but we are the only Armenians left here. I will send my boy to Istanbul. Someday we hope to go there, too."

Then he turned to me. "Your mother had a sister. She had two small daughters. In 1915, the little ones were taken in by a Turkish family. They live not far from here. If you can stay, I will take you to meet them."

If only I could talk to these people alone, I thought, *without the major, without anyone else present. Maybe I am causing them trouble by calling attention to them this way.*

Then the father said, "Would you like to see the cemetery? Your grandfather Gougas is buried there. The authorities moved the graves in the Christian cemetery a while ago, but I still know where he is buried. He was a fine man. I remember him from my youth."

The major then proposed that I stay on an extra day, and he would accompany me back to Sivas. My husband said he must go back to Ankara but also suggested I stay and visit with this Armenian family. I couldn't decide, so we made our way back to the town and went to the café for coffee. I hated myself for being so irresolute. When we were seated, I turned to the major.

"But, Major, what really happened? The whole world knows about the Armenian massacres. Did it happen in Zara too? You must know."

The major, a decent man, seemed to turn pale. "Massacres, no. It was wartime. This is our eastern border with Russia. The Armenians were traitors. Many Turks were killed too, you know."

"But women and children and old people?" It was not a question. I was unarmed. At that moment I felt a surge of emotion I had never before experienced. The conversation came to a standstill.

On the way back to Sivas, we were silent, but protocol demanded a gesture of civility in saying our farewells to the major. I couldn't blame him, but I did not want to see him again.

It was early August. Back in Ankara, it was dry, sooty, and like a furnace. I only wanted one thing—to go home, to see my mother once again. Before we departed, I sent a bundle of clothes off to the family we had visited, and many weeks later, when I arrived home, I found two letters from them. How sorry I am now that I didn't correspond with these kind people. They seemed so grateful to have at last established contact with some relatives or friends in America, so humble and careful not to ask for anything and so anxious to share what they had. They had suffered but were still trusting.

Zara, c. 1962
Photo courtesy Julian Kulski

A street in Zara, c. 1962

Leaving Zara, c. 1962

Hosanna's Account

I went directly to Los Angeles, where my mother was living. I hadn't seen her in a long time. She had shrunk and only came up to my shoulders. I recounted my journey to her. She listened in silence. Then she began to talk. I took notes, and this is the order in which she spoke:

When the war came, Esahog, who was married to my sister Miriam, was arrested and taken to jail in Sivas. You know, he was a talented person. He used to make floral decorations for buildings out of concrete-like material made with egg whites. He and my brother Antranig went together to the town of Yopag and made these for a Turkish family. He also made something of this kind for the military fort near the river in Zara. Later, he acquired the general store which Nishan Sherinian had turned over to Nishan Gagian, who in turn had bequeathed it to Esahag when he, Nishan, left for America. Esahag was a successful businessman. He had this store when the war came.

Miriam [her sister], Esahag's wife, was put on the road in the deportation. She died on the road from Harput.

Their two girls were supposedly taken in by a Turkish family. [These were the two that were still living outside Zara during my visit. I will everlastingly regret that I did not go to see them.]

Hovhannes (my father) was last seen in Zara in 1915. He was taken with other men from Zara by Turks to the surrounding hills and shot.

Gulvart (my mother) was put on the deportation road with the others out of Zara. She made it as far as Urfa, where people were rounded up and put in the church there, which was then set on fire. She is buried in a small place called Zraka. The Armenian Holy Cross Church [Catholic?] buried her there. Her son Ezekial's wife and baby were with her. The baby was buried with Gulvart.

Ezekial [my mother's brother] was seen once in Zara after the war by Yagout Gochian [my mother's aunt]. In

1915 he was taken by the Turks, supposedly to work on the roads. When the war came, my mother took the money out of his store and hid it in our farmhouse. She told a Turk neighbor where it was and said the neighbor could have it if she would save Ezekial's life when he returned. It is believed Turks took him to the farm, got the money, and then killed him.

Ezekial and his wife, Aznig Sherinian, had a boy who evidently died in Zara. She was put on the deportation road. She gave birth when they reached Urfa, and both died there. [This is the baby buried with Gulvart.]

Muketar, Hosanna's younger brother, thirteen at the time she left Zara, died in the war. How and where are not known.

Kirkor Kezerian [Hosanna's paternal uncle] was in jail in 1914 and presumably was killed by the Turks. He was a Mormon.

Propion, Kirkor's wife [Hosanna's aunt], was starving to death in Zara in 1915.

Yagout [Hosanna's aunt], was married to a Sahag Gochian, who died in Zara before the war. They had a son, and after the war, Yagout, the son, and his wife went to Leninakan. Yagout died there. She had a field near the river, which she sold to Turks after the war. A Turk who knew her had saved her.

We spent several hours this way, my mother and I. I asked how she knew all this, and she said it had been told to her by a lady who had been with the Zara people when they were deported and had survived. She had immigrated to Watertown, Massachusetts, and had written to my mother years later. Yes, she said, this was her testament.

"Why didn't you tell me all this before?" I asked.

"You were young, and you wouldn't understand," she said. "Besides, it wouldn't bring them back."

Hosanna's aunt Yagout and family, date unknown.

The same family in Leninakan, minus the elder, c. 1930s

ISABEL-ROSE KULSKI

John's Death

As it happened, the day I had gotten to Los Angeles to see my mother was also the day my two brothers, Sam and Art, arrived from the Salt Lake Valley, where they had gone to bury their father. They were both sad, especially Sam, who had always repressed his emotions but now had tears in his eyes. John had been harsh to him as a child, but no matter, both boys loved him.

John had been ailing for a long time, his lungs compacted with flue dust from the many years he had worked at the smelter. He had been living alone in the little company house close by the abandoned slag dump since the end of the war when the company cut back and eventually shut down the entire works. The old sampling mill and the two smokestack spires and buildings housing the furnaces were left abandoned, dust-covered industrial ghosts of an era that had come and gone. Many of the men who had worked there from the days when it had opened around the turn of the century through the First Great War until after the Second had long since passed on.

John had been one of the star performers there during the last war, putting in two shifts at a time, in the certain knowledge that his effort was not only going to help America win the war but to spur on the Soviet Union, of which the Armenia he called his homeland was a part, and our ally in those days. His belief, as if it was a religion, in a worker's utopia had probably sustained him through the years of toil. His sons would reap the rewards in the better world that would be brought about once all countries had acknowledged "the blessings of a Communist society"—at least that is what I thought he believed.

But then, how should I know? He was my "other father"—not really my father at all—and I scarcely knew him.

Revisiting the Zara Saints

We had taken pictures of the travels in Turkey, and so in the next few days, I had time to reflect on the trip and arrange these to show family. My mother was not very interested in them, just a little surprised that some of the things she remembered about her home and Zara were not there. Where was the big wooden door to her father's house? Where was the church they had gone to? I asked her if she would like to take a trip back there, not that it was likely I would ever return. She said no; what would be the purpose when there was no one there she would know? And so, the time passed quickly, and once again I said good-bye.

On the way home, I stopped in my valley and old home of Murray to visit with Arick and Armenak. They hadn't seen me in years, but they greeted me warmly. Arick had heard of my trip to Zara from my mother, and I thought since I was the first person to go back to the scenes of their youth, they would like to see the pictures of Turkey. Most of the places were unfamiliar to them, as they had never traveled in Turkey themselves, except to leave it. But I was something of a marvel for having been to Zara, which was now but a distant memory to them.

In November 1962, I received a letter from Arick, which had a pointed significance, now for it corroborated, with little differing detail, the account my mother gave me during my Los Angeles visit with her. The word had got around among the Zara Saints in the valley about my trip, even before my visit to Arick, and one day, a letter came from Mr. F. A. Gagosian, a relative of my mother on her mother's side:

> I would like to know how it happened that you went to Zara. What was your purpose? You mean to tell me that there are only 4 Armenian families in Zara altogether?

When it used to be 4 or 5 hundred families, please make this point clear when you write again.

I do not know anyone that came to this country after the 1915 massacre when lot of Armenians died with the Turkish sword. I had a lot of relatives die at that time, mostly from my mother's side.

Mr. Gagosian subsequently sent me a copy of the picture of the Zara Saints with identities. He invited me to return to Utah to get more of the information he had. He also wanted me to go back to Zara with him. Unfortunately, I did not pursue this correspondence or his suggestion, but I heard that after my visit, others went there.

Last Journeys

Farewell to Father: Virginia Interlude

It was late October. My father had been with me almost two months. He was unwell, still feeling the effects of the long journey from California and looking pale and gaunt. He could not get accustomed to the forest of trees of the Virginia landscape. He remarked how many trees there were and none of them bearing fruit. At home in the high country, trees had to be planted, watered, and cared for, and one expected fruit from all that labor.

All that September and into October, I had to leave him alone during the day when I went to work, but I was able on some days to come home at lunchtime to check up on him. We had a deep garden. At the end of it, I had made a small ivy bower at a higher elevation where one could sit in the shadows and look down the stone path through the shrubbery to the house. That was where I would usually find him, looking forlorn but happy when he saw me approach. The whole garden, in a sense, was a bower, with tall oaks surrounding it and a high hemlock hedge on each side. Sunshine did not penetrate except in the late afternoon, when there was mottled light here and there.

Day by day, my father's situation deteriorated. I managed to have a doctor call at the house. He diagnosed a prostate problem and, like an old-fashioned country doctor, taped him up with a catheter and told me his condition would only get worse. In those days, care for that affliction was not as advanced as it is now. I don't recall that an operation was recommended. I was at a loss what to do other than follow the doctor's advice. He didn't come often, and slowly my father succumbed to the toxins working in his body. One day, when the missionaries had found us, I thought, *now there will at least be some spiritual support*. They came several times, and as my father weakened further, I asked them to come with elders of the priesthood to give him a blessing, "calling," as they would say, "on the Lord to make him well again if that be His will."

My father was a deeply religious person. In Salt Lake, he had always, every Sunday of his life, gone to church. Now he was here in alien territory, away from all that had been home to him in America, and except for me and the missionaries, stranded among strangers. He liked the Mormon hymns and would sometimes sing them when he was alone. He would say the words from one that usually closed the service, "God be with you till we meet again." It was his way of saying good-bye. One day toward the end of October, he said he wanted to go home to see the sunshine again. I demurred, saying it would be too cold to go now, but I would take him in the spring. I did promise that, but in my heart, I knew I would not be making that journey with him.

He died the last day of October. It rained, and red leaves showered down in the garden.

I called my sisters in Los Angeles and made the arrangements for the funeral a few days hence. The body was to be transported in a pinewood coffin to Utah in the same plane I was traveling in. Past, present, and future seemed eternally enveloped in the long hours it took to get home. The members of the priesthood, men who to my father were his brothers, left their work on short notice and came to the service. It was held in the church where through all the trials of his life in America he had found a home. Each of the members bore witness to his kindness, his selflessness, and above all his allegiance to a path of Christian humbleness.

The rain that had started with our journey west did not stop, but it receded to a gentle mist when we reached the cemetery. There in the Elysian Gardens, a glistening emerald carpet at the base of the Wasatch Range, he was buried. Lying there at his side were two of those Saints from Zara, Antranig and Lucy Kezerian.

Arick asked the mourners to her home following the burial. Only a dozen or so people came. Arick and her husband, Armenak, were the only ones there to recall the old days from Zara. Out of place was one of our old neighbors, who asked if he could buy my father's cottage if it was for sale. My thoughts were miles away from that subject, but I said that it would not be sold.

A long interval later, when I went out to the valley again, I had a flat granite stone placed on my father's grave. I thought he would approve of the words carved on it: "Till we meet again."

The pioneer house was emptied of my father's belongings, including the knitting machine he had spent his winter days churning away at. Unoccupied, the house attracted wayfarers, including a Mexican family that lingered there for a time. The neighbor kept up a string of requests to buy the place, but each time I refused. Eventually, when my remaining sister Ruth wanted to sell, I succumbed, and it was sold for a song, and the house was torn down to make room for "progress." Now, with a concrete highway and warehouses covering the entire former Anderson Avenue, it is hard to even guess where it once stood.

My Mother: Last Chapters

My brother had established himself in business on Sunset Boulevard in Hollywood and eventually moved my mother up close to that area to a cottage-style house on a small lot with lovely aromatic pepper trees in front. There were many such houses along the old streets that were built in the early days of Hollywood, which had attracted master carpenters who built sets for the studios.

My brother found a succession of caregivers for my mother as she aged, and some of them were quite memorable. One was Sephora. She was Armenian and had come from Iraq, a quite attractive woman. Her husband, she said, had been a photographer in the Iraqi king's household in the old days before the revolution overthrew the monarchy. Why she had separated from her husband, where he was, what life she had lived before were all veiled in vague references to the court in Baghdad. But it was evident from this lady's appearance and manner that she had seen better times and had been accustomed to a sophisticated life. She was gone the next time I visited.

The last of the caregivers was another Armenian woman, this time from Armenia at the time when it was still under Soviet rule. This lady, Mrs. Aznik, had immigrated to the United States to join her relatives. She had left grown children behind and proudly showed pictures of them. At first, Mrs. Aznik seemed eager to please and willing to look after the house and to cook some native dishes for my mother. When I went on one of my trips to Los Angeles, she had picked up a little English, but she also kept contrasting "socialism" and its virtues, such as free education, with her life in America. "Well, if it was so great, why did you leave?" my mother asked.

This I write about not only as I recall it as the trials accompanying old age, but as the contrast between these Russian Armenians with those of the first immigrants whom the missionary Saints had sponsored, such as my father, to their valley of Zion. I have heard it said that in Turkey, Armenians stood to lose their lives, in Russia their souls. In America—thank God, I thought—they are free to reclaim both if they are able.

Between the various caregivers came an interval where no suitable person could be found to look after my mother, so she spent a few months in an Armenian old-age home outside of the city. It was at first an acceptable solution for her, as she was among contemporaries who spoke her language and were from the early immigration. They could exchange information about the people they had left behind when they came to America. Their first question was, "*Kaghat ut oour er?*" "Where was your town?" or "Where were you from?"

This was before the days when Armenian immigrants were beginning to arrive in greater numbers from the Soviet Union. Most of the residents at the home had migrated from Turkey, but there were now a number of young Armenian women who had come from Soviet Armenia and had found work at the home. They seemed different—more Russian than Armenian in their dress, their manners, even their speech. I think my mother liked the company of her compatriots, but the young women were taking advantage of the telephone she had in her room and were using it as a station for making all their long-distance calls to relatives or their local boyfriends and consequently giving her no peace.

I visited my mother there on two or three of my trips west, and each time I came away dissatisfied with the situation. So, I arranged with my brother to take her with me to my home in Virginia. Perhaps this was more to assuage my own feelings of not having done my share toward her care than a genuine conviction that she would be better off with me. As it was with the time when my father was with me, this interval turned out to be not so pleasant—it did not provide the quietude people seek whose days stretch out aimlessly as life ebbs away.

I wasn't able to give my mother the attention she should have had. I would take her to the Armenian church, her ancestral church, heavy with incense and doleful music, but this seemed irrelevant to her needs. The church membership at that time was predominantly made up of the second or third migration—people mainly from Middle Eastern countries who were more militant in their international outlook, imbued with what was called "small-nation chauvinism." They looked upon Armenia as the "homeland" as if it actually existed, even though at that time it was under the rule of Soviet Russia. This was far different from those early immigrants from Turkey who knew they were coming to a new homeland and whose ties with their past came to be forever terminated as the Armenians of Turkey were no more. It was a totally different outlook on who we now were and what we might become. There was no real place for my mother among these newer, so different immigrants.

I had not been so close to my mother in the early days when I had lived that peripatetic life between her home and my father's place, and even less so as time and space widened the separation between us. But now, as I cared for her, I developed an affection that I had not had before. She didn't talk much about the old days and hardly at all about the days of her youth and her own lost mother, her lost family in Zara. I wonder if they had faded from her memory, though I don't see how it could be, because even I, never having known or even seen a likeness of her mother, could not erase from my imagination the picture of this poor woman driven from a humble home on an endless journey on foot in that April of 1915 to death and unmarked burial. It was in those days when our roles were reversed and I would bathe my mother, wash her hair, and dress her that I would say to her, "You are my little girl now."

One evening, I thought it might give my mother a lift to talk with someone over old times in Murray, so I called her cousin Arick, the one person left who would remember her. Arick had said in her letter to me that she would like to be friends with my mother again. They talked by telephone for quite a while, sometimes in Armenian but mostly in their English. I couldn't hear what Arick was saying, but my mother concluded the conversation with, "Is that all there is? All of it seems like a dream now."

In times past, my mother had often said to me not to go and not to be where I was not wanted. I think she felt unwanted in my household. She had said as much in telephone conversations with my brother Art, and he had agreed that she could return to the house he had provided for her in the past. So, one day late in summer, we flew back, but the place was not yet ready for her, so we detoured to my sister Ruth's in the San Diego mountain country.

Sam, my other brother, retired now from his work for the navy, drove us there from the airport. It was hot and dry as we reached the town of Ramona, Indian country, then still a village with tall eucalyptus trees lining the main street and giving off their herbal fragrance in the faint afternoon breeze. Suddenly, my mother started to cry. Maybe it was exhaustion from the journey or the uncertainty of her future and her helplessness in the hands of her children. I didn't show it, but when I looked at her, small and defenseless, I felt tears inside too.

The stay at Ruth's place was brief. Ruth had made a mountain retreat out of a hardscrabble place. She had been fiercely independent ever since she had left Utah and was intent on remaining that way. As I knew from my early-childhood memory, there was a reserve of anger in her. I overheard it in her remarks to Hosanna. In my mother's time with me, when I had allowed myself to voice a barbed remark, I had seen the same look of silent anguish on my mother's face that I saw now. *We shouldn't have stopped her*, I thought to myself.

The next day, we set out through the back country for Los Angeles. I wish I could have known my mother's thoughts during those long, wordless hours on our way. I could not know it then, but this was to be the last chapter of her life, a chapter enveloped in the indignities dealt her by that last caregiver, a stranger from the other remote Eastern Armenia.

I went to see my mother every few months. After that talk with Arick, she no longer had any contact with any Zara people or with any Saints from our old home. Only she would know how often, if at all, she thought of those of her family who had come to America with her or those left behind and lost to history. But as the new America receded in her life, the old religion seemed to resurface.

Whenever anything went awry, she would say *"Der Voghormia,"* (Lord have mercy!) Her final words to me on my last trip to see her were *"Asdvadz kez byheh"* (God be with you).

She drew comfort in her final days that Art, her last child, was near her and came daily to cheer her up. She would give him detailed instruction about his health. She never gave up being a mother to him, and he, with his innate good nature, allowed her that pleasure with scarcely a murmur in her presence.

She died in the spring of 1979. The funeral was conducted at Saint James Armenian Apostolic Church in Los Angeles, with an Armenian priest officiating. I gave a short testimonial about her life, her Zara family, her sojourn to Utah, and the rest. Old Gougas, her grandfather, who had embraced the missionaries, might have preferred the presence there of Saints, but her parents, Hovhanes and Gulvart, would probably have felt satisfied with the emissary of the old religion.

Hosanna with her children
(Left to right) Standing: Art, Hosanna, Sam.
Seated: Isabel, Lily, Ruth.
Taken at the home of Lily Redfern, c. 1955

Going Home—A Sentimental Journey

Home is where the heart is. But you can't go there again, so it is said. Still, right now I'm on my way back to my father's pioneer cottage, high, high up in a mountain valley. I haven't been there in long years but I know it's all there because it exists in miniature detail in my mind.

I've come by train—the Denver and Rio Grande Western, to the old, ornate station. I'll make my way on foot across the rough part of town, which always seems to be west of the railroad tracks, to the bus that will take me all the way down the valley. It is winter. A heavy snow fell yesterday and is banked now five feet high along the roads. Bright sunshine has already melted little puddles along the road. The air is like a sheath of crystal brushing against my face, embracing me with unaccustomed magnetic energy. I say to myself, *I'm not going to be unhappy, no tears of remembrance, not today.*

As the bus, nearly empty, bumps along the road southward, I get my fill of the white spires that rim the eastern side of the valley. I recognize only the twin peaks that still gaze in silence down on the valley floor. I'll not stop at the little red brick house where she, estranged from my father and the world, had withdrawn in perpetual distress. It's empty now, or maybe strangers have found refuge there. I'll go on a few blocks to the bus stop in front of my old school.

Once there, I'll walk up the hill, snow crunching under my boots. The sidewalk and irrigation ditch along the road are buried deep in snow. It won't be long. I'll soon turn off at the lane bordering the railroad tracks. I hope it's plowed, or it will take me forever to get home to my dad. I trudge along on the tire tracks of a truck.

Now I will pause a moment at the junction along this lane, where the water in the ditch changes course. I can hear it gurgling under the snow. This is the place where I stopped again and again with my father on our walks to town. We would take off our shoes on a hot summer day and dig our feet in the arctic waters of the ditch. Here one day he said, "My heart is broke." He never said that again, but I still hear him. The ore-sampling mill is silent, its ancient machinery lined up against the shattered windows, a gray remnant of an industrial ghost.

I'll turn off now and walk the last half mile on the tracks. The sun has already melted the snow on the steel ribs stretching endlessly for parallel miles southward. I'll be there soon, and I know my dad will be home because I see a spiral of blue smoke rising from the chimney of his house, half obscured in snow. Even before I get to the door, a whiff of spicy aroma from the stew on his coal stove will welcome me.

I'll find him there. I know I will, even though a concrete freeway has buried his cottage, and the swift whirring cars drown out the cry of the gulls that fly high overhead across his home and the valley.

A page from Nishan's brief memoir.

The Saints of Zara. Members of the Mormon Church, 1901

ISABEL-ROSE KULSKI